Language, context, and text: aspects of language in a social-semiotic perspective

M. A. K. Halliday and Ruqaiya Hasan

Series Editor: Frances Christie

Oxford University Press
1989

Oxford University Press
Walton Street, Oxford OX2 6DP

Oxford   New York   Toronto
Delhi   Bombay   Calcutta   Madras   Karachi
Petaling Jaya   Singapore   Hong Kong   Tokyo
Nairobi   Dar es Salaam   Cape Town
Melbourne   Auckland

and associated companies in
Berlin   Ibadan

Oxford English and the *Oxford English* logo are trade marks of
Oxford University Press

ISBN 019 437154 9

© Deakin University 1985, 1989

First published 1985
Second edition 1989

Printed in Hong Kong.

About the authors

M.A.K. Halliday

Michael Halliday was born in Leeds, England, in 1925. He took his BA at London University in Chinese language and literature, then studied linguistics as a graduate student, first in China (Peking University and Lingnan University, Canton) and then at Cambridge, where he received his PhD in 1955.

After holding appointments at Cambridge and Edinburgh he went to University College London in 1963, as Director of the Communication Research Centre. There he directed two research projects, one in the Linguistic Properties of Scientific English and the other in Linguistics and English Teaching; the latter produced *Breakthrough to Literacy* for lower primary schools and *Language in Use* for secondary schools. In 1965 he was appointed concurrently Professor of General Linguistics, with responsibility for building up a new department in this subject. He remained at University College London until the end of 1970. From 1973 to 1975 he was Professor of Linguistics at the University of Illinois, Chicago Circle. At the beginning of 1976 he became Head of the new Department of Linguistics at the University of Sydney, the post that he now holds. He was consultant to the Curriculum Development Centre's Language Development Project 1976–78, and subsequently a member of the Project Review and Advisory Panel.

He taught on the Linguistic Society of America's summer Linguistic Institutes in 1964 (Indiana), 1966 (UCLA), and 1973 (Michigan), and was elected to honorary membership of the Society in 1978. He has held visiting professorships at Yale, Brown, UC. Irvine, and the University of Nairobi; and in 1972-73 was a Fellow of the Centre for Advanced Study in the Behavioural Sciences at Stanford, California. In 1969 he was awarded an honorary doctorate at the University of Nancy, France; and in 1981 he received the David H. Russell Award for Distinguished Research in the Teaching of English from the National Council of Teachers of English (USA).

His current research interests are the semantics and grammar of modern English; language development in early childhood; text linguistics and register variation; educational applications of linguistics; and artificial intelligence, in which he is associated with the 'Penman' project at the Information Sciences Institute, University of Southern California.

Ruqaiya Hasan

Ruqaiya Hasan was born in India. She took her BA degree from Allahabad University in English Literature, Education, and History. Then afer migrating to Pakistan, she took her MA degree in English Literature from the University of Punjab, Lahore. Teaching English Literature at this University, she found she needed a viable framework for the study of language in literature. This led her into linguistics, and she went to Britain and took a PhD in Linguistics at the University of Edinburgh. She has taught at the University of Edinburgh, University College London, and as a visiting scholar at University of California (Berkeley), University of Illinois (Urbana), Northwestern University (Evanston, Ill.), and the University of Essex. She started the Nuffield Child Language Survey at Leeds University in 1964, and after a period as Research Fellow in the Nuffield Programme in Linguistics and English Teaching at University College London, she joined Bernstein's Sociolinguistics Research Unit at the University of London Institute of Education, where she was responsible for the Nuffield Project in the Sociolinguistic Study of Children's Stories. She is currently Associate Professor in Linguistics at Macquarie University.

M.A.K. Halliday and Ruqaiya Hasan have both published widely in the field of systemic linguistics. In 1976, they co-authored *Cohesion in English* (Longman, London).

Foreword

In a sense, educational interest in language is not new. Studies of rhetoric and of grammar go back as far as the Greeks; in the English-speaking countries, studies of the classical languages, and more recently of English itself, have had a well established place in educational practice. Moreover, a number of the issues which have aroused the most passionate debates about how to develop language abilities have tended to remain, resurfacing at various points in history in somewhat different formulations perhaps, but nonetheless still there, and still lively.

Of these issues, probably the most lively has been that concerning the extent to which explicit knowledge about language on the part of the learner is a desirable or a useful thing. But the manner in which discussion about this issue has been conducted has often been allowed to obscure other and bigger questions: questions, for example, both about the nature of language as an aspect of human experience, and about language as a resource of fundamental importance in the building of human experience. The tendency in much of the western intellectual tradition has been to dissociate language and experience, in such a way that language is seen as rather neutral, merely serving to 'carry' the fruits of experience. Whereas in this view language is seen as a kind of 'conduit', subservient to experience in various ways, an alternative view, as propounded in the books in this series, would argue that language is itself not only a part of experience, but intimately involved in the manner in which we construct and organise experience. As such, it is never neutral, but deeply implicated in building meaning. One's notions concerning how to teach about language will differ quite markedly, depending upon the view one adopts concerning language and experience. In fact, though discussions concerning teaching about language can sometimes be interesting, in practice many such discussions have proved theoretically ill-founded and barren, serving merely to perpetuate a number of unhelpful myths about language.

The most serious and confusing of these myths are those which would suggest we can dissociate language from meaning — form from function, or form from 'content'. Where such myths apply, teaching about language becomes a matter of teaching about 'language rules' — normally grammatical rules — and as history has demonstrated over the years, such teaching rapidly degenerates into the arid pursuit of parts of speech and the parsing of isolated sentences. Meaning, and the critical role of language in the building of meaning, are simply overlooked, and the kinds of knowledge about language made available to the learner are of a very limited kind.

The volumes in this series of monographs devoted to language education in my view provide a much better basis upon which to address questions related to the teaching about language than has been the case anywhere in the English-speaking world for some time now. I make this claim for several reasons, one of the most important being that the series never sought directly to establish a model for teaching about language at all. On the contrary, it sought to establish a principled model of language, which, once properly articulated, allows us to address many questions of an educational nature, including those to do with teaching about language. To use Halliday's term (1978), such a model sees language primarily as a 'social semiotic', and as a resource for meaning, centrally involved in the processes by which human beings negotiate, construct and change the nature of social experience. While the series certainly does not claim to have had the last word on these and related subjects, I believe it does do much to set a new educational agenda — one which enables us to look closely at the role of language both in living and in learning: one which, moreover, provides a basis upon which to decide those kinds of teaching and learning about language which may make a legitimate contribution to the development of the learner.

I have said that arguments to do with teaching about language have been around for a long time: certainly as long as the two hundred years of white settlement in Australia. In fact, coincidentally, just as the first settlers were taking up their enforced residence in the Australian colony of New South Wales, Lindley Murray was preparing his *English Grammar* (1795), which, though not the only volume produced on the subject in the eighteenth century, was certainly the best. Hundreds of school grammars that were to appear in Britain and Australia for the next century at least, were to draw very heavily upon what Murray had written. The parts of speech, parsing and sentence analysis, the latter as propounded by Morell (an influential inspector of schools in England), were the principal elements in the teaching about language in the Australian colonies, much as they were in England throughout the century. By the 1860s and 1870s the Professor of Classics and Logic at Sydney University, Charles Badham, who had arrived from England in 1867, publicly disagreed with the examining authorities in New South Wales concerning the teaching of grammar. To the contemporary reader there is a surprising modernity about many of his objections, most notably his strongly held conviction that successful control of one's language is learned less as a matter of committing to memory the parts of speech and the principles of parsing, than as a matter of frequent opportunity for use.

Historically, the study by which issues of use had been most effectively addressed had been that of rhetoric, in itself quite old in the English-speaking tradition, dating back at least to the sixteenth century. Rhetorical studies flourished in the eighteenth century, the best known works on the subject being George Campbell's *The Philosophy of Rhetoric* (1776), and Hugh Blair's *Lectures on Rhetoric and Belles Lettres* (1783), while in the nineteenth century Richard Whately published his work, *Elements of Rhetoric* (1828). As the nineteenth century proceeded, scholarly work on rhetoric declined, as was testified by the markedly inferior but nonetheless influential works of Alexander Bain (*English Composition and Rhetoric*, 1866; Revised version, 1887). Bain, in fact, did much to corrupt and destroy the older rhetorical traditions, primarily because he lost sight of the need for a basic concern with meaning in language. Bain's was the century of romanticism after all: on the one hand, Matthew Arnold was extolling the civilising influence of English literature in the development of children; on the other hand, there was a tendency towards suspicion, even contempt, for those who wanted to take a scholarly look at the linguistic organisation of texts, and at the ways in which they were structured for the building of meaning. In 1921, Ballard (who was an expert witness before the Newbolt Enquiry on the teaching of English), wrote a book called *Teaching the Mother Tongue*, in which he noted among other things, that unfortunately in England at least rhetorical studies had become associated with what were thought to be rather shallow devices for persuasion and argument. The disinclination to take seriously the study of the rhetorical organisation of texts gave rise to a surprisingly unhelpful tradition for the teaching of literature, which is with us yet in many places: 'civilising' it might be, but it was *not* to be the object of systematic study, for such study would in some ill-defined way threaten or devalue the work of literature itself.

A grammarian like Murray had never been in doubt about the relationship of grammar and rhetoric. As he examined it, grammar was concerned with the syntax of the written English sentence: it was not concerned with the study of 'style', about which he wrote a short appendix in his original grammar, where his debt to the major rhetoricians of the period was apparent. Rhetorical studies, especially as discussed by Campbell for instance, did address questions of 'style', always from the standpoint of a recognition of the close relationship of language to the socially created purpose in using language. In fact, the general model of language as discussed by Campbell bore some relationship to the model taken up in this series, most notably in its commitment to register.

The notion of register proposes a very intimate relationship of text to context: indeed, so intimate is that relationship, it is asserted, that the one can only be interpreted by reference to the other. Meaning is realised in language (in the form of text), which is thus shaped or patterned in response to the context of situation in which it is used. To study language then, is to concentrate upon exploring how it is systematically patterned towards important social ends. The linguistic theory adopted here is that of systemic linguistics. Such a linguistic theory is itself also a social theory, for it proposes firstly, that it is in the nature of human behaviour to build reality and/or experience through complex semiotic processes, and secondly, that the principal semiotic system available to humans is their language. In this sense, to study language is to explore some of the most important and pervasive of the processes by which human beings build their world.

I originally developed the volumes in this series as the basis of two major off campus courses in Language Education taught in the Master's degree program at Deakin University, Victoria, Australia. To the best of my knowledge, such courses, which are designed primarily for teachers and teacher educators, are the first of their kind in the world, and while they actually appeared in the mid 1980s, they emerge from work in language education which has been going on in Australia for some time. This included the national Language Development Project, to which Michael Halliday was consultant, and whose work I co-ordinated throughout its second, productive phase. (This major project was initiated by the Commonwealth Government's Curriculum Development Centre, Canberra, in the 1970s, and involved the co-operation of curriculum development teams from all Australian states in developing language curriculum materials. Its work was not completed because of political changes which caused the activities of the Curriculum Development Centre to be wound down.) In the 1980s a number of conferences have been held fairly regularly in different parts of Australia, all of them variously exploring aspects of language education, and leading to the publication of a number of conference reports. They include: Frances Christie (ed.), *Language and the Social Construction of Experience* (Deakin University, 1983); Brendan Bartlett and John Carr (eds.), *Language in Education Workshop: a Report of Proceedings* (Centre for Research and Learning, Brisbane C.A.E., Mount Gravatt Campus, Brisbane, 1984); Ruqaiya Hasan (ed.), *Discourse on Discourse* (Applied Linguistics Association of Australia, Occasional Papers, Number 7, 1985); Clare Painter and J.R. Martin (eds.), *Writing to Mean: Teaching Genres across the Curriculum* (Applied Linguistics Association of Australia, Occasional Papers, Number 9, 1986); Linda Gerot, Jane Oldenburg and Theo Van Leeuwen (eds.), *Language and Socialisation: Home and School* (in preparation). All these activities have contributed to the building of a climate of opinion and a tradition of thinking about language which made possible the development of the volumes in this series.

While it is true that the developing tradition of language education which these volumes represent does, as I have noted, take up some of the concerns of the older rhetorical studies, it nonetheless also looks forward, pointing to ways of examining language which were not available in earlier times. For example, the notion of language as a social semiotic, and its associated conception of experience or reality as socially built and constantly subject to processes of transformation, finds very much better expression today than would have been possible before, though obviously much more requires to be said about this than can be dealt with in these volumes. In addition, a functionally driven view of language is now available, currently most completely articulated in Halliday's *An Introduction to Functional Grammar* (1985), which offers ways of understanding the English language in a manner that Murray's Grammar could not have done.

Murray's Grammar confined itself to considerations of the syntax of the written English sentence. It did not have anything of use to say about spoken language, as opposed to written language, and, equally, it provided no basis upon which to explore a unit other than the sentence, whether that be the paragraph, or, even more importantly, the total text. The preoccupation with the written sentence reflected the pre-eminent position being accorded to the written word by Murray's time, leading to disastrous consequences since, that is the diminished value accorded to spoken language, especially in educational practices. In Murray's work, the lack of a direct relationship between the study of grammar on the one hand, and that of 'style', on the other hand, was, as I have already noted, to be attributed to his view that it was the rhetorician who addressed wider questions relating to the text. In the tradition in which he worked, in fact, grammar looked at syntactic rules divorced from considerations of meaning or social purpose.

By contrast, Halliday's approach to grammar has a number of real strengths, the first of which is the fact that its basis is semantic, not syntactic: that is to say, it is a semantically driven grammar, which, while not denying that certain principles of syntax do apply, seeks to consider and identify the role of various linguistic items in any text in terms of their function in building meaning. It is for this reason that its practices for interpreting and labelling various linguistic items and groupings are functionally based, not syntactically based. There is in other words, no dissociation of 'grammar' on the one hand and 'semantics' or meaning on the other. A second strength of Halliday's approach is that it is not uniquely interested in written language, being instead committed to the study of both the spoken and written modes, and to an explanation of the differences between the two, in such a way that each is illuminated because of its contrast with the other. A third and final strength of the systemic functional grammar is that it permits useful movement across the text, addressing the manner in which linguistic patternings are built up for the construction of the overall text in its particular 'genre', shaped as it is in response to the context of situation which gave rise to it.

Halliday's functional grammar lies behind all ten volumes in this series, though one other volume, by Michael Christie, called *Aboriginal perspectives on experience and learning: the role of language in Aboriginal Education*, draws upon somewhat different if still compatible perspectives in educational and language theory to develop its arguments. The latter volume, is available directly from Deakin University. In varying ways, the volumes in this series provide a helpful introduction to much that is more fully dealt with in Halliday's Grammar, and I commend the series to the reader who wants to develop some sense of the ways such a body of linguistic theory can be applied to educational questions. A version of the grammar specifically designed for teacher education remains to be written, and while I cherish ambitions to begin work on such a version soon, I am aware that others have similar ambitions − in itself a most desirable development.

While I have just suggested that the reader who picks up any of the volumes in this series should find ways to apply systemic linguistic theory to educational theory, I want to argue, however, that what is offered here is more than merely a course in applied linguistics, legitimate though such a course might be. Rather, I want to claim that this is a course in educational linguistics, a term of importance because it places linguistic study firmly at the heart of educational enquiry. While it is true that a great deal of linguistic research of the past, where it did not interpret language in terms of interactive, social processes, or where it was not grounded in a concern for meaning, has had little of relevance to offer education, socially relevant traditions of linguistics like that from which systemics is derived, do have a lot to contribute. How that contribution should be articulated is quite properly a matter of development in partnership between educationists, teachers and linguistics, and a great deal has yet to be done to achieve such articulation.

I believe that work in Australia currently is making a major contribution to the development of a vigorous educational linguistics, not all of it of course in a systemic framework. I would note here the important work of such people as J.R. Martin, Joan Rothery, Suzanne Eggins and Peter Wignell of the University of Sydney, investigating children's writing development; the innovatory work of Brian Gray and his colleagues a few years ago in developing language programs for Aboriginal children in central Australia, and more recently his work with other groups in Canberra; the recent work of Beth Graham, Michael Christie and Stephen Harris, all of the Northern Territory Department of Education, in developing language programs for Aboriginal children; the important work of John Carr and his colleagues of the Queensland Department of Education in developing new perspectives upon language in the various language curriculum guidelines they have prepared for their state; the contributions of Jenny Hammond of the University of Wollongong, New South Wales, in her research into language development in schools, as well as the various programs in which she teaches; research being undertaken by Ruqaiya Hasan and Carmel Cloran of Macquarie University, Sydney, into children's language learning styles in the transition years from home to school; investigations by Linda Gerot, also of Macquarie University, into classroom discourse in the secondary school, across a number of different subjects; and the work of Pam Gilbert of James Cook University, Townsville, in Queensland, whose interests are both in writing in the secondary school, and in language and gender.

The signs are that a coherent educational linguistics is beginning to appear around the world, and I note with pleasure the appearance of two new and valuable international journals: *Language and Education*, edited by David Corson of Massey University, New Zealand, and *Linguistics in Education*, edited by David Bloome, of the University of Massachusetts. Both are committed to the development of an educational linguistics, to which many traditions of study, linguistic, semiotic and sociological, will no doubt make an important contribution. Such an educational linguistics is long overdue, and in what are politically difficult times, I suggest such a study can make a major contribution to the pursuit of educational equality of opportunity, and to attacking the wider social problems of equity and justice. Language is a political institution: those who are wise in its ways, capable of using it to shape and serve important personal and social goals, will be the ones who are 'empowered' (to use a fashionable word): able, that is, not merely to participate effectively *in* the world, but able also *to act upon it*, in the sense that they can strive for significant social change. Looked at in these terms, provision of appropriate language education programs is a profoundly important matter, both in ensuring equality of educational opportunity, and in helping to develop those who are able and willing to take an effective role in democratic processes of all kinds.

One of the most encouraging measures of the potential value of the perspectives open to teachers taking up an educational linguistics of the kind offered in these monographs, has been the variety of teachers attracted to the courses of which they form a part, and the ways in which these teachers have used what they have learned in undertaking research papers for the award of the master's degree. They include, for example, secondary teachers of physics, social science, geography and English, specialists in teaching English as a second language to migrants and specialists in teaching English to Aboriginal people, primary school teachers, a nurse educator, teachers of illiterate adults, and language curriculum consultants, as well as a number of teacher educators with specialist responsibilities in teaching language education. For many of these people the perspectives offered by an educational linguistics are both new and challenging, causing them to review and change aspects of their teaching practices in various ways. Coming to terms with a semantically driven grammar is in itself quite demanding, while there is often considerable effort involved to bring to conscious awareness the ways in which we use language for the realisation of different meanings. But the effort is plainly worth it, principally because of the added sense of control and direction it can give teachers interested to work at fostering and developing students who are independent and confident in using language for the achievement of various goals. Those people for whom these books have proved helpful, tend to say that they have achieved a stronger and richer appreciation of language and how it works than they had before; that because they know considerably more about language themselves, they are able to intervene much more effectively in directing and guiding those whom they teach; that because they have a better sense of the relationship of language and 'content' than they had before, they can better guide their students into control of the 'content' of the various subjects for which they are responsible; and finally, that because they have an improved sense of how to direct language learning, they are able to institute new assessment policies, negotiating, defining and clarifying realistic goals for their students. By any standards, these are considerable achievements.

As I draw this Foreword to a close, I should perhaps note for the reader's benefit the manner in which students doing course work with me are asked to read the monographs in this series, though I should stress that the books were deliberately designed to be picked up and read in any order one likes. In the first of the two semester courses, called *Language and Learning*, students are asked to read the following volumes in the order given:

Frances Christie — *Language education*
Clare Painter — *Learning the mother tongue*
M.A.K. Halliday & Ruqaiya Hasan — *Language, context, and text: aspects of language in a social-semiotic perspective*
J.L. Lemke — *Using language in the classroom*
then either,
M.A.K. Halliday — *Spoken and written language*
or,
Ruqaiya Hasan — *Linguistics, language, and verbal art.*

The following four volumes, together with the one by Michael Christie, mentioned above, belong to the second course called *Sociocultural Aspects of Language and Education*, and they may be read by the students in any order they like, though only three of the five need be selected for close study:

David Butt — *Talking and thinking: the patterns of behaviour*
Gunther Kress — *Linguistic processes in sociocultural practice*
J.R. Martin — *Factual writing: exploring and challenging social reality*
Cate Poynton — *Language and gender: making the difference*

References

Bain, A., *An English Grammar* (Longman, Roberts and Green, London, 1863).

Bain, A., *English Composition and Rhetoric*, revised in two Parts — *Part 1, Intellectual Elements of Style*, and *Part 11, Emotional Qualities of Style* (Longman, Green and Company, London, 1887).

Ballard, P., *Teaching the Mother Tongue* (Hodder & Stoughton, London, 1921).

Blair, H., *Lectures on Rhetoric and Belles Lettres, Vols. 1 and 11* (W. Strahan and T. Cadell, London, 1783).

Campbell, G., (new ed.), *The Philosophy of Rhetoric* (T. Tegg and Son, London, 1838). Originally published (1776).

Halliday, M.A.K., *Language as social semiotic: the social interpretation of language and meaning* (Edward Arnold, London, 1978).

Halliday, M.A.K., *An Introduction to Functional Grammar* (Edward Arnold, London, 1985).

Murray, Lindley, *English Grammar* (1795), Facsimile Reprint No. 106 (Menston, Scolar Press, 1968).

Contents

Part A
M.A.K. Halliday

Chapter 1
Context of situation

Introduction

Our general approach to the study of language, as our title is intended to suggest, is one that focuses upon the social: upon the social functions that determine what language is like and how it has evolved. Let me begin by saying a few words about both parts of our overall title.

Language in a social-semiotic perspective

The phrase 'language in a social-semiotic perspective' characterises the sort of approach that we have been following in our recent work, and which, I think, has been a feature of my own thinking ever since I became interested in the study of language. The term 'social-semiotic' can be thought of as indicating a general ideology or intellectual stance, a conceptual angle on the subject. But at the same time there is a more specific implication to be read into both of these terms, semiotic and social.

The concept of **semiotics** derives initially from the concept of the sign; and the modern word harks back to the terms *semainon*, *semainomenon* ('signifier, signified') used in ancient Greek linguistics by the Stoic philosophers. The Stoics were the first to evolve a theory of the sign, in the 3rd–2nd century BC; and the conception they had of the linguistic sign was already well advanced along the lines in which it was developed two thousand years later in the work of Ferdinand de Saussure.

For a good account of Saussure's ideas, see Jonathan Culler (1976).

Semiotics can therefore be defined as the general study of signs. But there is one limitation that has usually been apparent in the history of this conception of the sign, and that is that it has tended to remain rather an atomistic concept. The sign has tended to be seen as an isolate, as a thing in itself, which exists first of all in and of itself before it comes to be related to other signs. Even in the work of Saussure, despite his very strong conception of language as a set of relationships, you will still find this rather atomistic conception of the linguistic sign. For that reason, therefore, I would wish to modify this definition of semiotics

semiotics

3

and say that, rather than considering it as the study of signs, I would like to consider it as the study of sign systems—in other words, as the study of **meaning** in its most general sense.

Linguistics, then, is a kind of semiotics. It is an aspect of the study of meaning. There are many other ways of meaning, other than through language. Language may be, in some rather vague, undefined sense, the most important, the most comprehensive, the most all-embracing; it is hard to say exactly how. But there are many other modes of meaning, in any culture, which are outside the realm of language.

These will include both art forms such as painting, sculpture, music, the dance, and so forth, and other modes of cultural behaviour that are not classified under the heading of forms of art, such as modes of exchange, modes of dress, structures of the family, and so forth. These are all bearers of meaning in the culture. Indeed, we can define a culture as a set of semiotic systems, a set of systems of meaning, all of which interrelate.

But to explain this general notion, we cannot operate with the concept of a sign as an entity. We have to think rather of **systems** of meaning, systems that may be considered as operating through some external form of output that we call a sign, but that are in themselves not sets of individual things, but rather networks of relationships. It is in that sense that I would use the term 'semiotic' to define the perspective in which we want to look at language: language as one among a number of systems of meaning that, taken all together, constitute human culture.

Secondly there is the term **social**, which is meant to suggest two things simultaneously. One is 'social' used in the sense of the social system, which I take to be synonymous with the culture. So when I say 'social-semiotic', in the first instance, I am simply referring to the definition of a social system, or a culture, as a system of meanings. But I also intend a more specific interpretation of the word 'social', to indicate that we are concerned particularly with the relationships between language and social structure, considering the social structure as one aspect of the social system.

social system

When we consider what realities there are that lie above and beyond language, which language serves to express, there are many directions in which we can move outside language in order to explain what language means. For some linguists (e.g., Chomsky, 1957; Lamb, 1966), the preferred mode of interpretation is the psychological one, in which language is to be explained in terms of the processes of the human mind or the human brain. For other linguists, perhaps, the direction might be a psychoanalytic one, or an aesthetic one, or any one of a number of possible perspectives. For us, then, the perspective primarily adopted— not to the exclusion of the others, but because this is where we look first to seek our explanations for linguistic phenomena—is the social one. We attempt to relate language primarily to one particular aspect of human experience, namely that of social structure.

Language is understood in its relationship to social structure.

Why this particular angle? It is not that we are excluding other

V is both psych.
social psych.

4

directions as irrelevant; but that for the questions we are interested in, especially educational questions, the social dimension seems particularly significant—and it is the one that has been the most neglected in discussions of language in education. Learning is, above all, a social process; and the environment in which educational learning takes place is that of a social institution, whether we think of this in concrete terms as the classroom and the school, with their clearly defined social structures, or in the more abstract sense of the school system, or even the educational process as it is conceived of in our society. Knowledge is transmitted in social contexts, through relationships, like those of parent and child, or teacher and pupil, or classmates, that are defined in the value systems and ideology of the culture. And the words that are exchanged in these contexts get their meaning from activities in which they are embedded, which again are social activities with social agencies and goals.

Language, context, and text

The main part of our title reflects our view that the way into understanding about language lies in the study of texts. The terms, CONTEXT and TEXT, put together like this, serve as a reminder that these are aspects of the same process. There is text and there is other text that accompanies it: text that is 'with', namely the con-text. This notion of what is 'with the text', however, goes beyond what is said and written: it includes other non-verbal goings-on—the total environment in which a text unfolds. So it serves to make a bridge between the text and the situation in which texts actually occur. Within our general topic, we shall be focusing on the special area of what in linguistics is referred to as a text; but always with emphasis on the situation, as the context in which texts unfold and in which they are to be interpreted.

texts defined

Let me try, then, to explain both these notions a little further. What do we mean by text, and what do we mean by context? I am going to do this in the opposite order: that is to say, I am going to talk about context first, for the reason that, in real life, contexts precede texts. The situation is prior to the discourse that relates to it.

Yes to a point but the precise nature of the situation is often defined by the discourse.

Malinowski and the notion of context of situation

It could be argued, in fact, that there was a theory of context before there was a theory of text. I have in mind here the work of the anthropologist Bronislaw Malinowski (1923, 1935), and in particular his theory of the context of situation. It is in that sense, or a closely related sense, that we shall be using the term 'context'.

Malinowski's context of situation

Much of Malinowski's research was undertaken in a group of islands of the South Pacific known as the Trobriand Islands, whose inhabitants lived mainly by fishing and gardening. Their language is referred to as Kiriwinian. Malinowski, who as well as being a great anthropologist was also a gifted natural linguist, found himself at an early stage able to converse freely in this language, and he did all his fieldwork among the island people using their own language. He then came to the problem of how to interpret and expound his ideas on the culture to English-speaking readers. He had many texts in Kiriwinian, texts that he had taken down in discussion with the Trobrianders; and the problem was how to render these in English in such a way as to make them intelligible. The culture that he was studying was, naturally, as different as it was possible to be from the culture that is familiar to Westerners.

In presenting the texts, Malinowski adopted various methods. He gave a free translation, which was intelligible, but conveyed nothing of the language or the culture; and a literal translation, which mimicked the original, but was unintelligible to an English reader. His principal technique, however, was to provide a rather extended commentary. This commentary, clearly, was not the same thing as the kind of commentary that a classical philologist engages in when he or she edits and translates some ancient written text. Rather it was the kind of commentary that placed the text in its living environment. Up to that time, the word 'context' in English had meant 'con-text'; that is to say, the words and the sentences before and after the particular sentence that one was looking at. Malinowski needed a term that expressed the total environment, including the verbal environment, but also including the situation in which the text was uttered. So with some apologies, in an article written in 1923, he coined the term CONTEXT OF SITUATION (Malinowski 1923). By context of situation, he meant the environment of the text.

the term 'context of situation' coined for this pupose

pragmatic and narrative contexts of situation

For example, Malinowski studied the language used in a fishing expedition when the islanders went in their canoes outside the lagoon into the open sea to fish; when they had caught a cargo of fish, they had the problem of navigating a rather difficult course through the reefs and back into the lagoon. As they came in, they were constantly in communication with those on the shore. They could shout instructions to each other, and they were, so to speak, talked in, in the way that an aircraft is talked down when it is coming in to land. Furthermore, there was an element of competition, a race between the different canoes.

This kind of language was very much pragmatic language. It was language in action, in which it was impossible to understand the message unless you knew what was going on, unless you had some sort of audio-video record of what was actually happening at the time. So Malinowski provided this account in his work. He described the fishing expedition. He described the return of the canoes and the way in which the people in the boats and the people on the shore were interacting with each other.

But he also saw that it was necessary to give more than the immediate environment. He saw that in any adequate description, it was necessary to provide information not only about what was happening at the time but also about the total cultural background, because involved in any kind of linguistic interaction, in any kind of conversational exchange, were not only the immediate sights and sounds surrounding the event but also the whole cultural history behind the participants, and behind the kind of practices that they were engaging in, determining their significance for the culture, whether practical or ritual. All these played a part in the interpretation of the meaning. So

Malinowski introduced the two notions that he called the context of situation and the CONTEXT OF CULTURE; and both of these, he considered, were necessary for the adequate understanding of the text.

context of culture

In some instances, his texts were severely pragmatic. That is to say, they were language used for the purpose of facilitating and furthering a particular form of activity, something that people were doing, exactly in the same way as we use language ourselves if we are engaged in some co-operative effort: suppose, for example, that the car has broken down and we are trying to repair it, and there are two or three people involved and they are shouting instructions to each other and giving advice and probably getting angry as well—the language is all part of the immediate situation.

But there were other types of text in which the reference was not so immediate and the function was not so directly pragmatic. For example, Malinowski observed many occasions when in the evenings the members of the group would gather around and listen to stories. Like most narratives, these stories were not related directly to the immediate situation in which they were told. As far as the subject-matter was concerned, it was irrelevant whether they were being told in the morning or in the evening, outside or inside, or what the particular surroundings were. The context in one sense was created by the stories themselves.

And yet in another sense, as Malinowski saw, even these narrative texts were very clearly functional. They had a creative purpose in the society; they had their own pragmatic context, and could be related to the situation in a slightly less direct manner. Often the telling of a story was related in some way or other to the continuing solidarity and well-being of the group. For example, during the season of the year when food was scarce, and famine was always a threat, they would tell stories about great famines in the past and how the people had united to overcome them. So the setting was not irrelevant; a story might be associated with a particular accredited story-teller, or a particular place or set of circumstances. In other words, there was still a context of situation, although it was not to be seen as a direct relation between the narrative line and the immediate surroundings in which the text was unfolding.

When Malinowski first developed these notions, he had the idea that you needed the concept of context of situation only if you were studying a 'primitive' language, the language of an unwritten culture, but that you would not need such concepts for the description of a language of a great civilisation. But over the next ten years or so, he came to the conclusion that he had been wrong; and he was an honest enough scholar to say so. He wrote, referring to his earlier work:

> I opposed civilised and scientific to primitive speech, and argued as if the theoretical uses of words in modern philosophic and scientific writing were completely detached from their pragmatic sources. This was an error, and a serious error at that. Between the savage use of words and the most abstract and theoretical one there is only a difference of degree. Ultimately all the meaning of all words is derived from bodily experience.
>
> (Malinowski, 1935, vol.2, p. 58).

The general notion of context of situation is as necessary for the understanding of English or any other major language as it is for the understanding of Kiriwinian. It is simply that the specific contexts of the culture are different. The activities that people are engaging in may differ from one place or one time to another; but the general principle that all language must be understood in its context of situation is just as valid for every community in every stage of development.

Malinowski was not primarily a linguist. He was not mainly concerned with explaining the Kiriwinian language or language in general, although he has some very perceptive things to say about language. He was an ethnographer, concerned to explain the culture. But in the course of his work, he had become deeply interested in language as an object of study in its own right.

linguistics as the study of meaning

At London University he had as a young colleague the linguist J.R. Firth, who subsequently became the first professor of general linguistics in a British university. Firth was interested in the cultural background of language, and he took over Malinowski's notion of the context of situation and built it in to his own linguistic theory. In Firth's view, expressed in an article he wrote in 1935, all linguistics was the study of meaning and all meaning was function in a context (Firth, 1935).

In one sense, however, Firth found that Malinowski's conception of the context of situation was not quite adequate for the purposes of a linguistic theory, because it was not yet general enough. Malinowski had been concerned with the study of specific texts, and therefore his notion of the context of situation was designed to elucidate and expound the meaning of particular instances of language use. Firth needed a concept of the context that could be built into a general linguistic theory: one which was more abstract than that, not simply an audio-video representation of the sights and sounds that surrounded the linguistic event. He therefore set up a framework for the description of the context of situation that could be used for the study of texts as part of a general linguistic theory.

Firth's description of context of situation

Firth's headings were as follows:

- the PARTICIPANTS in the situation: what Firth referred to as persons and personalities, corresponding more or less to what sociologists would regard as the statuses and roles of the participants;
- the ACTION of the participants: what they are doing, including both their VERBAL ACTION and their NON-VERBAL ACTION
- OTHER RELEVANT FEATURES OF THE SITUATION: the surrounding objects and events, in so far as they have some bearing on what is going on;
- the EFFECTS of the verbal action: what changes were brought about by what the participants in the situation had to say.

Firth outlined this framework in 1950, and perhaps the best application of it is in a study done by Firth's former colleague Professor T.F. Mitchell, subsequently professor of linguistics at Leeds. Mitchell studied the 'language of buying and selling', the language of transactions in shops and markets and auctions, which he observed in North

Africa. The language studied is Arabic. In his article on the subject, Mitchell (1957) works out and illustrates very well Firth's ideas regarding the nature of the context of situation of a text.

Since that time, there have been a number of other outlines or schemata of this kind by which linguists have set out to characterise the situation of a text. The best known is probably that of the American anthropologist Dell Hymes.

. . . exemplified by Mitchell from the 'language of buying and selling' in northern Africa

Dell Hymes and the ethnography of communication

In his work in the ethnography of communication, Dell Hymes (1967) proposed a set of concepts for describing the context of situation, which were in many ways similar to those of Firth. He identified:

- the form and content of the message;
- the setting;
- the participants;
- the intent and effect of the communication;
- the key;
- the medium;
- the genre;
- the norms of interaction.

Hymes' work led to a renewal of interest in the different ways in which language is used in different cultures—the value placed on speech, the various rhetorical modes that are recognised, and so on.

Important books that arose out of this interest are Cazden et al. (1972) and Bauman & Sherzer (1974).

Determining the most appropriate model of the context of situation

There are certain principles that we can use for choosing an appropriate way of describing the context of a situation of a text. They relate to the fact, a rather important fact, that people do on the whole understand each other. We are always hearing in linguistics, and more especially from our colleagues in other fields such as literature, or media and communication studies, about failures of communication, reflecting what is a very genuine concern with this problem in contemporary societies. And indeed failures do occur. But rather than being surprised at the failures, given the complexity of modern cultures, it seems to me we should be surprised at the successes. What is remarkable is how often people do understand each other despite the noise with which we are continually surrounded. How do we explain the success with which people communicate?

The short answer, I shall suggest, is that we know what the other person is going to say. We always have a good idea of what is coming next, so that we are seldom totally surprised. We may be partly surprised; but the surprise will always be within the framework of something that we knew was going to happen. And this is the most important phenomenon in human communication. We make predictions—not consciously, of course; in general, the process is below the level of awareness—about what the other person is going to say next; and that's how we understand what he or she does say.

success in communication

What the linguist is concerned with is: how do we make these predictions? The first step towards an answer is: we make them from the context of situation. The situation in which linguistic interaction takes place gives the participants a great deal of information about the meanings that are being exchanged, and the meanings that are likely to be exchanged. And the kind of description or interpretation of the context of situation that is going to be the most adequate for the linguist is one that characterises it in those terms; that is, in terms that enable him or her to make predictions about meanings, of a kind that will help to explain how people interact.

In Chapter 2 below we shall suggest a simple framework for describing the context of situation in a way that links it up with the expectations people have of what others are likely to say. Before this, however, we should say more clearly what we mean by the term 'text'.

What a text is

What do we mean by text? We can define text, in the simplest way perhaps, by saying that it is language that is functional. By functional, we simply mean language that is doing some job in some context, as opposed to isolated words or sentences that I might put on the black-board. (These might also be functional, of course, if I was using them as linguistic examples.) So any instance of living language that is playing some part in a context of situation, we shall call a text. It may be either spoken or written, or indeed in any other medium of expression that we like to think of.

text as meaning

The important thing about the nature of a text is that, although when we write it down it looks as though it is made of words and sentences, it is really made of meanings. Of course, the meanings have to be expressed, or coded, in words and structures, just as these in turn have to be expressed over again—recoded, if you like—in sounds or in written symbols. It has to be coded in something in order to be communicated; but as a thing in itself, a text is essentially a semantic unit. It is not something that can be defined as being just another kind of sentence, only bigger.

A text is a semantic unit.

Thus, we cannot simply treat a theory of text as an extension of grammatical theory, and set up formal systems for deciding what a text is. It is by no means easy to move from the formal definition of a sentence to the interpretation of particular sentences of living language; and this problem is considerably greater in the case of the text. Because of its nature as a semantic entity, a text, more than other linguistic units, has to be considered from two perspectives at once, both as a product and as a process. We need to see the text as product and the text as process and to keep both these aspects in focus. The text is a product in the sense that it is an output, something that can be recorded and studied, having a certain construction that can be represented in systematic terms. It is a process in the sense of a continuous process of semantic choice, a movement through the network of meaning potential, with each set of choices constituting the environment for a further set.

text as product and as process

One method of describing a text is by exegesis, or *explication de texte*, a kind of running commentary on the product that reveals something of its dynamic unfolding as a process. The problem for this approach is that you need to look beyond the words and structures so as to interpret the text as a process in a way that relates it to the language as a whole. The commentary embodies no conception of the linguistic system that lies behind that text; and yet without the system, there would be no text. On the other hand, it is also necessary to describe the system of the language in such a way that it is conceivable that people could use it. Some attempts to devise a theory of language have done so in a way that makes it almost inconceivable that anybody could have used that system to produce a text. The problem for linguistics is to combine these two conceptions of the text, as product and as process, and to relate both to the notion of the linguistic system that lies behind them.

Now, with the sort of social-semiotic perspective that we are adopting here, we would see the text in its 'process' aspect as an interactive event, a social exchange of meanings. Text is a form of exchange; and the fundamental form of a text is that of dialogue, of interaction between speakers. Not that dialogue is more important than other kinds of text; but in the last resort, every kind of text in every language is meaningful because it can be related to interaction among speakers, and ultimately to ordinary everyday spontaneous conversation. That is the kind of text where people exploit to the full the resources of language that they have; the kind of situation in which they improvise, in which they innovate, in which changes in the system take place. The leading edge of unconscious change and development in any language is typically to be found in its natural conversational texts—in this context of talk as the interpersonal exchange of meanings.

[margin note: text as a social exchange of meanings or "co-construction"]

A text, then, is both an object in its own right (it may be a highly valued object, for example something that is recognised as a great poem) and an instance—an instance of social meaning in a particular context of situation. It is a product of its environment, a product of a continuous process of choices in meaning that we can represent as multiple paths or passes through the networks that constitute the linguistic system. But of course any general characterisation of that kind is useful only if it enables us to describe specific instances. We must be able to characterise this or that particular text in such a way as to be able to relate it to this general concept. And at this point, I would like to give an example of one way in which it may be possible to define the context of situation of a text.

Let me return for a moment to the semiotic concept of meanings that are created by the social system—that in a sense constitute the social system—which are exchanged by the members of a culture in the form of text. The text, we have said, is an instance of the process and product of social meaning in a particular context of situation. Now the context of situation, the context in which the text unfolds, is encapsulated in the text, not in a kind of piecemeal fashion, nor at the other extreme in any mechanical way, but through a systematic relationship between the social environment on the one hand, and the functional organisation of language on the other. If we treat both text and context as

[margin note: relationship of social environment and functional organisation of language]

11

semiotic phenomena, as 'modes of meaning', so to speak, we can get from one to the other in a revealing way.

So let us pick up the questions, 'how can we characterise a text in its relation to its context of situation?' and 'how do we get from the situation to the text?'. This will then lead us to a consideration of how people make predictions about the kinds of meaning that are being exchanged.

The three features of the context of situation

I would like to give you two brief illustrations, each comprising a short English text together with a description of the context of situation in which it functioned (see Texts 1.1 and 1.2). The description is in terms of a simple conceptual framework of three headings, the field, the tenor, and the mode. These concepts serve to interpret the social context of a text, the environment in which meanings are being exchanged.

1. The FIELD OF DISCOURSE refers to what is happening, to the nature of the social action that is taking place: what is it that the participants are engaged in, in which the language figures as some essential component?

2. The TENOR OF DISCOURSE refers to who is taking part, to the nature of the participants, their statuses and roles: what kinds of role relationship obtain among the participants, including permanent and temporary relationships of one kind or another, both the types of speech role that they are taking on in the dialogue and the whole cluster of socially significant relationships in which they are involved?

3. The MODE OF DISCOURSE refers to what part the language is playing, what it is that the participants are expecting the language to do for them in that situation: the symbolic organisation of the text, the status that it has, and its function in the context, including the channel (is it spoken or written or some combination of the two?) and also the rhetorical mode, what is being achieved by the text in terms of such categories as persuasive, expository, didactic, and the like.

field—what is happening
tenor—who are taking part
mode—what part the language is playing

Text 1.1 is a legal document that can be used when someone is buying or selling a house; it is in a very simple form—they are usually much longer than this—but it is valid as a legal document, and you will immediately recognise it as a legal document. An interpretation of its context of situation is set out underneath. It is a document relating to a recognised social transaction, namely the exchange of immovable property. It is a formulaic text used by a 'member' to address the 'collective' with reference to some specific instance. And it is written to be filed away in somebody's filing cabinet as a document giving validity to the transaction. Moreover, it is performative in the sense that the text actually constitutes or realises the act in question.

12

Text 1.1

Transfer of whole (Freehold or Leasehold)

Title number—SY 43271604

Property—14 Twintree Avenue, Minford

In consideration of ten thousand five hundred pounds the receipt whereof is hereby acknowledged

   I, Herbert William Timms, of (address)

as beneficial owner hereby transfer to:

   Matthew John Seaton, of (address)

the land comprised in the title above mentioned. It is hereby certified that the transaction hereby effected does not form part of a larger transaction or series of transactions in respect of which the amount or value or aggregate amount or value of the consideration exceeds twelve thousand pounds.

Signed, sealed and delivered by the said Herbert William Timms in the presence of (witness)

Situational description:

Field: Verbal regulation of social interaction through sanctions of the legal system:
codification of exchange of property ('deed of transfer'), including certification that transaction falls within particular class of transactions defined by value of commodity exchanged

Tenor: 'Member' (individual) addressing 'collective' (society) using formula prescribed by collective for purpose in hand

Mode: Written to be filed (i.e. to form part of documentary records); text gives status (as social act) to non-verbal transaction; text is formulaic (i.e. general, with provision for relating to specific instances)
Performative (i.e. text constitutes, or 'realises', act in question).

The three headings of field, tenor, and mode enable us to give a characterisation of the nature of this kind of a text, one which will do for similar texts in any language. But we can use the same general headings for the description of a text of any kind. Text 1.2 is a little passage from a broadcast talk that was given in England some years ago, by a distinguished churchman concerned with the status of Christianity in the modern world.

Text 1.2

(from a radio talk by the Bishop of Woolwich)

The Christian should therefore take atheism seriously, not only so that he may be able to answer it, but so that he himself may still be able to be a believer in the mid-twentieth century. With this in mind, I would ask you to expose yourself to the three thrusts of modern atheism. These are not so much three types of atheism—each is present in varying degree in any representative type—so much as three motives which have impelled men,

13

particularly over the past hundred years, to question the God of their up-bringing and ours. They may be represented by three summary statements:

God is intellectually superfluous;
God is emotionally dispensible;
God is morally intolerable.

Let us consider each of them in turn.

Situational description:

Field: Maintenance of institutionalised system of beliefs; religion (Christianity), and the members' attitudes towards it; semi-technical

Tenor: Authority (in both senses, i.e. person holding authority, and specialist) to the audience; audience unseen and unknown (like readership), but relationship institutionalised (pastor to flock)

Mode: Written to be read aloud; public act (mass media: radio); monologue; text is whole of relevant activity
Lecture; persuasive, with rational argument

The field is thus the maintenance of an institutionalised system of beliefs: the nature of the Christian religion, and of people's attitudes towards it, at a semi-technical level. The tenor is that of an authority to an audience. He is an authority in both senses: he holds authority in the Church, as a bishop, and he is an authority on religion, a theologian. He cannot see the audience, and does not know them; but his relationship to them is institutionalised in the culture, as that of pastor to flock. The mode is that of a text that was written in order to be read aloud, as a public act on the mass media; it was a monologue, in which the text itself was the whole of the relevant activity—nothing else significant was happening. And it is a persuasive discussion, based on rational argument.

In Chapter 3, I shall return to the second of these examples, in order to suggest the reasons for setting up this particular framework for representing the 'situation' of a text. As in a great deal of linguistics, the aim is to be able to state consciously, and to interpret, processes that go on unconsciously all the time, in the course of daily life—in other words, to represent the system that lies behind these processes. In this instance, the process we are interested in is that of producing and understanding text in some context of situation, perhaps the most distinctive form of activity in the life of social man.

Chapter 2
Functions of language

Introduction

What do we understand by the notion 'functions of language'? In the simplest sense, the word 'function' can be thought of as a synonym for the word 'use', so that when we talk about functions of language, we may mean no more than the way people use their language, or their languages if they have more than one. Stated in the most general terms, people do different things with their language; that is, they expect to achieve by talking and writing, and by listening and reading, a large number of different aims and different purposes. We could attempt to list and classify these in some way or other, and a number of scholars have attempted to do this, hoping to find some fairly general framework or scheme for classifying the purposes for which people use language.

There are a number of familiar classifications of linguistic functions: for example, that put forward by Malinowski, which is associated with his work on situation and meaning referred to earlier. Malinowski (1923) classified the functions of language into the two broad categories of pragmatic and magical. As an anthropologist, he was interested in practical or pragmatic uses of language on the one hand, which he further subdivided into active and narrative, and on the other hand in ritual or magical uses of language that were associated with ceremonial or religious activities in the culture.

Malinowski's functions: pragmatic and magical

A quite different classification is that associated with the name of the Austrian psychologist Karl Bühler (1934), who was concerned with the functions of language from the standpoint not so much of the culture but of the individual. Bühler made the distinction into expressive language, conative language, and representational language: the expressive being language that is oriented towards the self, the speaker; the conative being language that is oriented towards the addressee; and the representational being language that is oriented towards the rest of reality—that is, anything other than speaker or addressee.

Bühler's functions: expressive, conative, and representational

Bühler was applying a conceptual framework inherited from Plato: the distinction of first person, second person, and third person. This in turn is derived from grammar (its source was in the rhetorical grammar that came before Plato)—based on the fact that the verbal systems in many European languages (including ancient Greek) are organised around a category of person, comprising first person, the speaker; second person, the addressee; and third person, everything else. On this basis, Bühler recognised three functions of language according to their orientation to one or other of the three persons. His scheme was adopted by the Prague School and later extended by Roman Jakobson (1960), who added three more functions: the poetic function, oriented towards the message; the transactional function, oriented towards the channel; and the metalinguistic function, oriented towards the code.

Britton's functions: transactional, expressive, and poetic

Bühler's scheme was adapted and developed in a different direction by the English educator James Britton (1970), who proposed a framework of transactional, expressive, and poetic language functions. Britton was concerned with the development of writing abilities by children in school, and held the view that writing developed first in an expressive context, and the ability was then extended 'outwards' to transactional writing on the one hand and to poetic writing on the other. Transactional language was that which emphasised the participant role, whereas in poetic language the writer's role was more that of spectator.

Morris's functions: information talking, exploratory talking, grooming talking, mood talking

Desmond Morris (1967), in his entertaining study of the human species from an animal behaviourist's point of view, came up with yet another classification of the functions of language, which he called 'information talking', 'mood talking', 'exploratory talking', and 'grooming talking'. The first was the co-operative exchange of information; Morris seemed to imply that that came first, although in the life history of a human child it arises last of all. The second was like Bühler's and Britton's 'expressive' function. The third was defined as 'talking for talking's sake; aesthetic, play functions'; while the fourth was 'the meaningless, polite chatter of social occasions'—what Malinowski had referred to forty years earlier as 'phatic communion', meaning communion through talk, when people use expressions like 'nice day, isn't it?' as a way of oiling the social process and avoiding friction.

Although these schemes look very different, and all use different terms, and although apart from Britton, none of the proponents had read any of the others, there is a considerable similarity among them, which we can bring out by tabulating them in a single display. Figure 2.1 sets them out in rows, in such a way that there is a vertical correspondence: each entry corresponds more or less to those above and below it. When we do this, we can see that they all recognise that language is used for talking about things (informative—narrative—representational), and they all recognise that language is used for 'me and you' purposes, expressing the self and influencing others (mood—expressive—conative—active). More patchily, there is then a third motif of language in a more imaginative or aesthetic function.

Function as a fundamental principle of language

What such scholars were doing was essentially constructing some kind of a conceptual framework in non-linguistic terms, looking at language

Figure 2.1 Functional theories of languages, where function equals 'use'

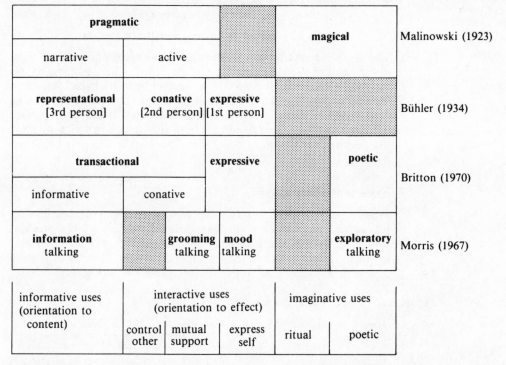

Note: shaded portions represent uses not covered by the author in question

from the outside, and using this as a grid for interpreting the different ways in which people use language. In all these interpretations of the functions of language, we can say that function equals use: the concept of function is synonymous with that of use. But in order to pursue our own investigations, we have to take a further step: a step that interprets functional variation not just as variation in the use of language, but rather as something that is built in, as the very foundation, to the organisation of language itself, and particularly to the organisation of the semantic system.

In other words, function will be interpreted not just as the use of language but as a fundamental property of language itself, something that is basic to the evolution of the semantic system. This amounts to saying that the organisation of every natural language is to be explained in terms of a functional theory.

function as a fundamental property of language

What I should like to do here is to illustrate the functional basis of language through the analysis of a single sentence. This is a risky thing to do, because there is always the danger that some incidental features that are the property of a particular sentence will be taken as if they are representative features of grammar in general. Of course, the features that are displayed in any particular sentence can only be incidental in relation to the linguistic system as a whole: they are the

17

ones that were chosen in this instance. So in interpreting a sentence, we try to relate what we say about it to general categories that are found in the grammar of the language.

Let us consider the following sentence:

Or leave a kiss within the cup, and I'll not ask for wine.

This is a sentence from a well-known English poem of the early seventeenth century (Ben Jonson: 'To Celia'). It is not the first line, as can be readily imagined. It is in fact the second line; but I shall not fill in the first line just for the moment. I want to try and perform some kind of an analytical commentary on that sentence; not, however, as a piece of literary analysis, but rather as a linguistic exercise in which we identify features that illustrate the general point—the functional basis of language.

Experiential meaning

First, then, let us look at this sentence from the point of view of what it is about—its meaning as the expression of some kind of a process, some event, action, state, or other phenomenal aspect of the real world to which it bears some kind of symbolic relation. If we take it more or less at its face value, it can be interpreted as in Figure 2.2.

Figure 2.2 Experiential structure

or	leave	a kiss	within the cup, and	I	'll	not	ask for	wine
'you' doer	'leave' action	'kiss' thing	'in cup' place	'I' doer		polarity: negative	'demand' verbal-isation	'wine' thing
Actor	Process	Goal	Locative	Sayer			Process	Range

Consider the word *leave*. If we take this by itself, we shall interpret it as some kind of a process, more particularly perhaps some kind of an action. Then there is the *kiss*, which is presumably some kind of a thing, although it is not very clear just what kind of a thing it is, and is the domain or sphere of influence of the action. Connected with these is *in + cup*, which is some kind of a circumstantial element, presumably a locative element, a place. So we have the representation of an action, a thing that is acted upon, and a place. We might also feel that we have to supply for ourselves somebody who is actually going to perform this action. So let us put in—in the gloss, because it is not overtly realised in the language—something we might call a doer, somebody who is going to do the deed.

Similarly in the second half: there is *wine*, which is a certain kind of a thing. There is *ask for*, which we may take as a single element; this is a process, but a different kind of process from the other one, since if you ask for something, you are going to use some kind of a signal, probably a linguistic signal, for the purpose. Let us call it a verbal process. There is also a doer; but the doer is present this time in *I*. Again, this is a different kind of doer; instead of being an actor, he is one who is engaging in a verbal process—or not engaging in it, since it is in fact negated. Let us call him a sayer.

18

So at the simplest level, the sentence can be regarded as a representation of some composite phenomenon in the real world. We know that there exist things like cups and wine. We know that when we speak, we become persons—'I' and 'you', and we have some interpretations for these. We know that there are processes of demanding, and of leaving. We can even perhaps do something with this notion of 'a kiss', though that is a 'thing' of a different kind from the wine, because although it is coded grammatically as a noun, it is normally the name of an action, not the name of an object. However, if it is something that can be left in a cup, then presumably at some level of interpretation, we have to see it also as an object. the sentence as an expression of meanings of different kinds

So far we have taken only one step in interpreting this sentence as a representation of some recognisable phenomenon. But we have isolated from this sentence certain features that can be thought of as representing the real world as it is apprehended in our experience. These could be said to display the EXPERIENTIAL meaning of that sentence. Clearly, we shall have to add to this some further component that will take us into the realm of an imaginative or oblique representation of experience—another step in the interpretation that allows us to explain this rather quaint conceit of 'leave a kiss within the cup'. experiential meaning

We could refer to this as metaphorical, extending the term to mean any instance of representation that involves a transfer—the kind of transfer, for example, that is present here in what is really a double shift in the meaning of the word *kiss*, because the word *kiss* as a noun is already metaphorical in the sense that it is the name for a process rather than for an object. That first metaphorical step is one that is built into the English language. Here however there is a second step, a special use of the word *kiss* involving a return at a higher level to the concept embodied in the fact that the word *kiss* is a noun. Nouns typically stand for objects, and objects can be left around the place; so you can 'leave a kiss within the cup'. It has taken us two steps to reach this point, each one involving a kind of metaphorical transfer.

If we continue this line of reasoning one step at a time, we shall be able to build up a complex chain of metaphorical realisations, leading to the interpretation of this sentence as representing what we would code in a less metaphorical, more direct way as something like *your kisses are more desirable than wine*, and more directly still, perhaps, as *I like to kiss you more than I like to drink wine*. Even that, of course, is by no means the end of the story, because we then have to pursue the modes of expression and the literary conventions that determine that this wording is an appropriate way of giving a particular message; but in order to do that, we will have to shift away from the experiential mode of meaning into another one, and look at the same sentence from a rather different point of view.

19

Interpersonal meaning

Consider Figure 2.3.

Figure 2.3 Interpersonal structure

or	leave a kiss within the cup and		I	'll not	ask for wine

'you'	'do that'
Subject	Residue

command: request

'I'	'voluntarily'	'do this'
Subject	Finite	Residue

offer: undertaking

In the first half we recognise something that signals a request: 'I request you to do this'. In the simplest semantic terms this is a variant of the general speech function of command. If we now look at the second half, we recognise the meaning 'I will not do that', or in other words 'I undertake not to do that'; and this is something that we could code in the most general terms as an offer. So we have the basic speech functions of command and offer.

Here we are looking at quite a different aspect of the meaning of that sentence. We are not now considering it from the point of view of its function in the representation of our experience. We are considering it from the point of view of its function in the process of social interaction. It is being interpreted not as a mode of thinking but as a mode of doing. The meaning is 'I request you to do something, and I undertake not to do something else'. Hence, a different kind of meaning is encoded in the same sentence, a kind of meaning that we will refer to as INTERPERSONAL meaning. The sentence is not only a representation of reality; it is also a piece of interaction between speaker and listener. Whereas in its experiential meaning language is a way of reflecting, in its interpersonal meaning language is a way of acting; we could in fact use that terminology, and talk about LANGUAGE AS REFLECTION and LANGUAGE AS ACTION as another way of referring to experiential and interpersonal meaning.

interpersonal meaning

Notice that, in analysing the grammar, we now need to recognise another distinct set of elements. We are not now analysing in terms of participants and processes; we are using the concept of a subject, and other related elements not shown here. So in the second clause we have the subject 'I', and in the first clause we have the subject 'you': 'you leave a kiss within the cup, and I will not ask for wine'.

The logical meaning

If we put the two interpretations together, the experiential and the interpersonal, we can account for each clause separately; but we still have to account for the 'and'. In other words, these two halves of the sentence are related in some way. Now the form of the relationship looks like a simple co-ordination of one thing with another: you (do) leave a kiss 'and' I (do not) ask for wine. But the two halves have a different

20

speech function. The one is a command, and more specifically a request; the other is an offer. What is the meaning of the co-ordination of a request and an offer? Clearly this is something that we have to reinterpret as something other than a simple co-ordination of like elements. Normally when one co-ordinates (a) and (b), then (a) and (b) belong to the same class. Here (a) and (b) do not belong to the same class. One is a command, the other is an offer. What is the effect of their co-ordination? The effect is that we need to reinterpret them in terms of some other relationship, one that typically in English we would express not paratactically, as here, but hypotactically by the use of an 'if'. So the next step we need to take is to recognise that not only is there a metaphor in the experiential meaning, but there is also a metaphor in the interpersonal meaning, because something that has been coded as 'request plus offer' is in fact going to be interpreted as 'offer conditional on acceptance of request'. We could express this as *if you leave a kiss within the cup, then I will not ask for wine*. So the interpersonal meaning is 'if you (agree to) do this, then I will (undertake) not (to) do that'.

But in order to take this step, we have had to invoke a third function of language, a third aspect of the organisation of the semantic system, namely its expression of fundamental LOGICAL relations. There is in every natural language a relatively small network of fundamental logical relations, which are not the relationships of formal logic, but are those from which the relationships of formal logic are ultimately derived. The logical relationships that are built into natural languages are those that are expressed in the grammar as different forms of parataxis and hypotaxis. So in our example the third component, which we will have to take account of in order to explain this relationship between the two parts, is the logical element which represents the meaning 'if . . . then . . .': 'if you leave a kiss within the cup, then I will not ask for wine'.

logical meaning

We have now taken a number of steps in the interpretation of this line, towards an explanation of how it means what it does. If at this point we go back and pick up the gloss that I gave earlier, 'your kisses are more desirable than wine'; now that we have included the active, interpersonal component in the meaning, we can personalise this and reinterpret the line more adequately as 'I value your kisses more than wine'. We can then instate 'kiss' and 'wine' as processes: 'I like to kiss you (even) more than I like to drink wine'; and this reinterpretation serves as a way in to the final metaphor whereby the wording stands as a declaration of love.

There is, in addition, another instance of a logical relation in the line—the 'or' that links it paratactically with what has preceded it. However, we have not yet considered the overall texture. We have not looked at this line from the point of view of its property as discourse. In order to do that, we shall need a context; so to begin with we must fill in the first line of the poem before it:

Drink to me only with thine eyes And I will pledge with mine
Or leave a kiss within the cup   And I'll not ask for wine

Now we notice a number of additional features of this text:

1. The pattern of 'you do (x) and I will do (y)' is in fact repeated on both occasions. So 'I request you to (do that) and I will (do this)'— and again the meaning is 'if': 'if you only drink to me with your eyes, then I will pledge with mine', paralleled by 'if you leave a kiss within the cup, then I will not ask for wine'. In both cases, there is the same pattern, a request followed by an offer, in both cases standing for an offer conditional on the acceptance of a request. This repetition is itself one aspect of the texture.

2. There is the thematic organisation of these two lines. In each case the speech function is signalled at the very beginning of the clause, which makes it stand as the theme. It is like announcing at the start 'what I am about to say is a request', or whatever it is going to be. This congruence of theme with mood is in no way unusual; in fact it is the typical pattern with offers and commands, where the speaker nearly always begins with the element that announces the mood. (The fact that it is typical does not make it less significant to the texture.)

3. Another component in the texture depends on rhythm and intonation, for which we shall have to assume a particular way of reading the line. I would say it as follows (the single or double slash marks a foot boundary; the caret marks a silent beat):

    //ˆ or / leave a / **kiss** wi//thin the / **cup**//ˆ and / I'll not / ask for / **wine** //

If you accept that reading, then we have three points of prominence: *kiss*, *cup*, and *wine*. Of course, this poem is more familiar to most English people as a song, since it was set to music, than as something to be spoken. But if it is spoken naturally without the music, then these are the likely places where the prominence would fall.

   This kind of prominence is a feature of the phonological system of modern English, in which any passage of spoken discourse is broken up into a succession of tone groups, or melodic units, each having one melodic contour (these are indicated by the double slash (//) in the example above). The tone group is not simply a unit of sound; it expresses a unit of meaning, one block of information in the total message. In every information unit, there is one point of prominence, the tonic nucleus (shown here by bold type); the prominence is also phonological—it is the segment with the greatest melodic movement—but again it expresses a prominence in meaning: it signals the focus of the information in the unit. This information focus marks the climax of new (either fresh or contrastive) information. So the two patterns—the division into information units, and the location of focus within each—together constitute a fundamental element in the texture of the spoken language.

4. The text is in fact a line of verse, and therefore has an idealised rhythm by virtue of belonging to a particular genre. In other words, it has a metre, determined by the particular verse form of which it is an instance. Here is the metric structure, set out in traditional form:

/ or leave / a kiss / within / the cup / and I'll / not ask / for wine / ˛ /

—except that in traditional metrics it would be said to have seven feet, whereas actually it has eight, because there is a silent one at the end. It is an eight-foot iambic line with one silent foot; and this metric pattern is another aspect of its texture. The 'true' rhythm of the line is a product of the tension between its metric structure and the natural rhythm that it would have in conversational spoken English.

We could if we wished go one stage further and analyse the line in terms of its intonation when spoken aloud. Again there would be the tension between the tone contours of natural speech and the melodic properties of its musical setting.

All these features—the semantic and grammatical balance between the lines, the thematic structure, the rhythm and information focus, and the metric structure—represent different aspects of the texture of the line. We refer to this as its TEXTUAL meaning. The textual meaning is what makes it into a text, as distinct from an artificial or fossilised specimen of wording.

textual meaning

To sum up, we have now identified four different aspects of the meaning of this line. These are, in fact, the four components in the semantics of every language, and in order to be able to use these concepts we shall need to be able to talk about them, and hence to give them names. We shall refer to them as:

four components of the semantics of every language

- experiential
- interpersonal
- logical
- textual

These strands of meaning are all interwoven in the fabric of the discourse. We cannot pick out one word or one phrase and say this has only experiential meaning, or this has only interpersonal meaning. What we had to do in analysing our text was to go back each time over the whole sentence and examine it again from a new point of view.

This is an important point to make, because there has been a lot of misunderstanding of the concept of the functions of language. It has often been assumed that each sentence has just one, or at least one primary, function; or, even if the sentence is recognised to be multifunctional, that it ought to be possible to point to each separate part of the sentence and to say this part has this function, that part has that function, and the other part has the other function.

But life in general is not like that, and language is certainly not like that. Every sentence in a text is multifunctional; but not in such a way that you can point to one particular constituent or segment and say this segment has just this function. The meanings are woven together in a very dense fabric in such a way that, to understand them, we do not look separately at its different parts; rather, we look at the whole thing simultaneously from a number of different angles, each perspective contributing towards the total interpretation. That is the essential nature of a functional approach.

language is multifunctional

23

The relationship of the text and its context of situation

Before we finish with this line, let us now look at it from the point of view of the function of the whole thing in a wider context, adopting the point of view that I was discussing in Chapter 1 when I spoke of the relationship between the text and the context of situation. We may be able to say a little about this line, and by implication about the whole poem, in terms of the notions of the FIELD, the TENOR, and the MODE. What can we say about it under these headings?

field

As far as the field of discourse is concerned—the general sense of what it is on about—clearly we could say that it is a love poem; in the broadest terms, therefore, the field of discourse is love. But it is love expressed as a metaphor, using the notions of drink and pledge.

tenor

Our second heading, the tenor of discourse, is concerned with the personal relationships involved: who are the participants in this text? Clearly, in the broadest terms it is man to woman, and more specifically lover to beloved. We should add, however, that there is a sub-motif here, because this is a poem; and that is that it is a public text. At what point in its existence it became a public text we do not necessarily know. It might have been performed as a public text right from the start. This was after all a recognised genre that was very fashionable at the beginning of the seventeenth century. On the other hand it might first of all have been written as a love poem by the poet to his mistress before it saw the light of day as a public text. Whichever is the case, it has a secondary tenor, that of a poet addressing his contemporaries.

mode

Thirdly, as far as the mode of discourse is concerned, that is to say the particular part that the language is playing in the interactive process, in the first instance we are treating it as a spoken text. It is also, of course, a written document; so let us say spoken/written. We could characterise it in more detail as, perhaps, written down in order to be spoken aloud. But we also have to say that it is composed, as distinct from spontaneous. It is a composition in a recognised genre involving highly elaborated modes of expression, somewhat self-conscious, and often referred to as 'conceits': imaginative metaphors, some of them (though not all) striking us as very far-fetched. This is, in turn, the product of a particular stage in the socio-cultural history of England in the post-Elizabethan period.

What can we say about the relationship between these headings, the field, the tenor, and the mode, and the particular linguistic features that are found in the poem? We can see that the field—the fact that it is a love poem, with the concept of love realised metaphorically in this way—is reflected most simply in the vocabulary, in the naming of processes and participants. It is reflected in the use of the words *drink* and *pledge* and *cup* and *wine* and *eyes* and *kiss*. And these embody two basic notions. They embody on the one hand the motif of drink, in the words *drink* and *pledge* and *cup* and *wine*; and on the other hand the motif of love, in particular, the *eyes* and the *kiss*. And there is of course a complex interaction between these two motifs, embodied in the notion of the cup that is touched with the mouth like a kiss and the eyes that meet over the cup as in love.

But the field of discourse is not only reflected in the vocabulary; it is also embodied in the transitivity structures in the grammar: in the verbal processes of *pledge* and *ask for* and in the processes of *drink* and *kiss*—but not, you will notice, *drink* + wine or *kiss* + person. These are not transitive structures in the poem: there is no object for the drink or the kiss.

Now, if we look at this pattern more closely, we can see that the contextual features that we entered under the 'field' of discourse are by and large reflected in just one of the modes of meaning of the poem, namely that which we referred to as the 'experiential' mode. So there is some kind of systematic relationship between the two, such that we can say that **the field is expressed through the experiential function in the semantics**.

Secondly, if we consider the tenor of discourse, which has to do with the relationship of man to woman, specifically lover to mistress, and the poet to contemporaries, how is this aspect of the context expressed? On the one hand, through the choice of 'person' in the grammatical sense: 'I', and 'you'. Those were the only Subjects in these two lines: 'you' then 'I' then 'you' then 'I'. And on the other hand, through the choice of speech function: command (specifically, a request) and offer (specifically an undertaking). The command is realised grammatically as an imperative clause: *drink to me only with thine eyes, leave a kiss within the cup*. The offer is realised grammatically as a declarative, with Subject *I* plus the modal *will: I will pledge with mine, I'll not ask for wine*.

These represent the tenor, the personal relationships that are involved, with their encoding in an elaborate metaphor as 'you do this and I'll do that, or you do this and I'll do that'. And this in turn stands as a symbolic representation of the conventional relationship that is always present in this genre, the convention of the reluctant mistress, the one who has to be persuaded and cajoled. So just as we were able to recognise certain lexico-grammatical features as particularly reflecting the field, namely those that we identified as carrying the experiential meaning, so also we can recognise other lexico-grammatical features as particularly reflecting the tenor, namely those that we identified as carrying the interpersonal meanings. In other words, **the tenor is expressed through the interpersonal function in the semantics**.

Finally, when we come to the mode of discourse, that of lyric poetry in a genre associated with the metaphysical poets, this clearly determines, apart from the metric pattern, also the choice of the themes. It is a general feature of lyric poetry that it is strongly person-oriented in its themes, so that typically the poet and the person spoken to are thematic—'I' and 'you' come first. Moreover the poem is clearly a self-contained text; this is reflected in the strong internal texture, in the balance that we noticed between the first two pairs of clauses. All these features together reflect the mode. Once again, therefore, we can make a general observation that the mode is typically reflected in lexico-grammatical features that we were able to identify as carrying the textual meanings. **The mode is expressed through the textual function in the semantics**.

Summarising these last few paragraphs, we can formulate the relationship between the situation and the text as in Figure 2.4.

Figure 2.4 Relation of the text to the context of situation

SITUATION: Feature of the context	(realised by)	TEXT: Functional component of semantic system
Field of discourse (what is going on)		Experiential meanings (transitivity, naming, etc.)
Tenor of discourse (who are taking part)		Interpersonal meanings (mood, modality, person, etc.)
Mode of discourse (role assigned to language)		Textual meanings (theme, information, cohesive relations)

Functions and meanings in a text

The kind of pattern we have found in our line of verse, whereby we could relate the elements of the context to the components of meaning in the text in a systematic way, is not just an artifact of that particular text, but is, in fact, a general feature of all texts. For an example of a text of a very different kind, let us look again at the extract from the broadcast talk given by the Bishop of Woolwich. This was a discussion of the nature of Christian belief and of the defence of this belief in the face of twentieth-century atheism; and we characterised its field, tenor, and mode in the following terms:

See Text 1.2, pp. 13–14.

Field: Maintenance of institutionalised system of beliefs; religion (Christianity), and the members' attitude towards it; semi-technical

Tenor: Authority (in both senses, i.e. person holding authority, and specialist) to the audience; audience unseen and unknown (like readership), but relationship institutionalised (pastor to flock)

Mode: Written to be read aloud; public act (mass media: radio); monologue; text is whole of relevant activity
Lecture; persuasive, with rational argument.

Let us see what there is in this text that reveals the various features of its context. Relating to the field, we have again most obviously the vocabulary—words in their function as names. There are lexical items expressing the meaning of Christianity and the maintenance of beliefs: not only the terms *God* and *Christian*, but also *atheism* and *believer* and expressions such as *motives impelling [one] to question*. There are also words to do with attack, and with resistance under attack. The military metaphor is foregrounded, as it always has been in Christian writings, where the concept of the embattled Christian is to the fore; so there is the word *thrust*, and if we added in the next two sentences following the extract, we should find the words *defence* and *advance* and *surrender*.

But once again it should not be implied that the experiential meaning is carried solely by the vocabulary. Words, in their function as names, are really an aspect of the transitivity patterns in the grammar, the types of process that are being talked about; and it is these that really carry the experiential meaning. In this text, as one would expect from looking at the field of discourse, we find mainly two kinds of process:

1. On the one hand there are the mental processes reflecting what is a highly thoughtful piece of discourse, processes expressed by words such as *take seriously*, *answer*, *expose oneself to*, *question*, and *consider*. The importance of these is not the particular words so much as the fact that they are all expressions of a single kind of process in the language, namely that type of mental process which implicitly can be verbalised. They are thoughts that can be said aloud. It is their function in the semantic system of English that is foregrounded here.

2. The second kind of process found in this text, again as is to be expected, is the relational process: the argument centres around problems of existence and attribution, and these are expressed through relational processes with verbs such as *represent* and *be*. So the field of discourse is clearly seen in the patterns of transitivity, which are the primary linguistic expressions of the experiential function.

The tenor, as we saw, is that of the pastor to the flock; this is typically reflected in the sequence 'I ask you (to do something)' and then 'let us (do something together)'. In other words, the interaction is of the form 'Here I am, the pastor. There are you, the flock. I am inviting you to do something; but I want you to see this as something that we are involved in together. So let us . . . (consider these in turn)'. And this same motif is continued in subsequent passages, where the speaker refers, for example, to *their upbringing and ours*; here *ours* means 'yours and mine', an inclusive *we* being intended.

Then there is the mood, the expression of speech function in the grammar, which shows an interesting pattern. The Bishop speaks as an authority; and he is, as I pointed out, an authority in both senses of the term. He is a specialist: that is, an academic authority, a theologian. But he is also a pastoral leader, an authority in the Church. His role as a specialist is encoded in declarative clauses, where the sense is 'this is how things are, and this is the explanation'. His role as a leader is encoded in imperative clauses, where the sense is 'this is what you (and I) should do about it'; and indirect imperatives of various kinds (for example, *The Christian should take atheism seriously*). So the overall impact is twofold: 'This is the situation; I tell you as a specialist. This is what should be done; I tell you as a leader'. So again the tenor, the relationship between the speaker and his audience, is reflected in grammatical patterns that express what we call the interpersonal meanings.

Finally the mode is that of a written text—written to be spoken aloud, but very carefully written. It is extremely simple grammatically, and extremely dense lexically. This combination is a feature of formal written language; it is the opposite of spontaneous spoken language, which tends to be grammatically complex and lexically sparse.

This point is taken up more fully in *Spoken and Written Language* (Halliday, 1989).

This text is characterised by simple grammatical structures, with an immense amount of lexical material packed into them. It is also a rational argument. So it proceeds through conjunctives: *therefore*, *with this in mind*, *in turn*, *first*, *next*, and so forth. It is highly textured, but mainly through its particular kind of cohesion.

Where there is anaphoric reference, as there always is in any textured material, it is typically anaphoric to the text. In other words, when the words *these* and *they* and *them* occur, they refer not to people or to things, but to passages in the preceding argument; and this is characteristic of closely argued, rational discourse. So once again, the mode, the particular part that the language is playing in the total event—the nature of the medium, and the rhetorical function—are reflected in what we have called the textual meanings, including the cohesive patterns.

This, I think, stated in its simplest terms, is the way in which speakers make predictions about the meanings that are to be exchanged, which was the point that I started from in the first section. Imagine that you come in, as we often do in real life, to a situation that is already going on. It does not matter what it is. It could be just a group of people engaged in any kind of activity. You, as an individual, come into this group from outside. Very quickly, you are able to take part in the interaction. How do you do this? You do it, I suggest, by constructing in your mind a model of the context of situation; and you do so in something like these terms. You assign to it a field, noting what is going on; you assign to it a tenor, recognising the personal relationships involved; and you assign to it a mode; seeing what is being achieved by means of language. You make predictions about the kinds of meaning that are likely to be foregrounded in that particular situation. So you come with your mind alert, with certain aspects of your language ready foregrounded, ready to be accessed, as it were, for taking part in this interaction. Something like this, I think, must be going on. Otherwise, it would be impossible to explain how it is that in real life we do so readily join in and take part in a situation that previously we knew nothing about.

Chapter 3
Register variation

Introduction

In the earlier chapters, I sought to develop a number of theoretical arguments. These could be summarised as follows:

1. The notion of 'context of situation'. This can be interpreted by means of a conceptual framework using the terms 'field', 'tenor', and 'mode': or, more fully expressed, field of discourse, tenor of discourse, and mode of discourse. These were the abstract components of the context of situation, if we look at it semiotically, as a construction of meanings.
2. The notion of 'functions of language'. These may be identified as the functional components of the semantic system of a language: (a) ideational, subdivided into logical and experiential; (b) interpersonal; and (c) textual.
3. The systematic relationship between the two. There is a correlation between the categories of the situation and those of the semantic system, such that, in general terms, the field is reflected in the experiential meanings of the text, the tenor in the interpersonal meanings, and the mode in the textual meanings. We could express this the other way round by using a complementary metaphor and saying that experiential meanings are activated by features of the field, interpersonal meanings by features of the tenor, and textual meanings by features of the mode.

These were discussed briefly in relation to Text 1.2. I propose now to discuss them more fully in relation to another text, Text 3.1, because this is an example where we can see very clearly the relationship between the situational and linguistic categories.

Linguistic and situational features of context

Nigel, aged 1 year 11 months, plays with a wooden train on the floor while he talks to his father.

Text 3.1

Nigel: [small wooden train in hand, approaching track laid along a plank sloping from chair to floor]
Here the ràilway line . . . but it not for the trāin to go on that.

Father: Isn't it?

Nigel: Yeš tís . . . I wonder the train will carry the lòrry.
[puts train on lorry (*sic*)]

Father: I wonder.

Nigel Oh yes it wíll . . . I don't wànt to send the train on this flóor . . . you want to send the train on the ràilway line [runs train up plank to chair] . . . but it doesn't go very well on the chāir [makes train go round in circles]. The train all round and ròund . . . it going all round and ròund . . . [tries to reach other train] have that tráin . . . have the blue tráin [= 'give it to me'; F. gives it to him] . . . send the blue train down the ràilway line . . . [plank falls off chair] lèt me put the railway line on the cháir [= 'you put the railway line on the chair!'; F. does so] . . . [looking at blue train] Daddy put sèllotape on it ['previously'] . . . there a very fierce lìon in the train . . . Daddy go and see if the lion still thére . . . Have your éngine ['give me my engine!'].

Father: Which engine? The little black engine?

Nigel: Yes . . . Daddy go and find it fór you . . . Daddy go and find the black éngine for you.

Intonation: ` = falling tone; ´ = rising tone; ˜ = falling-rising tone. Tonic nucleus falls on syllables having tone marks; tone group boundaries within an utterance shown by . . .

Situation

Field: Child at play: manipulating movable objects (wheeled vehicles) with related fixtures, assisted by adult; concurrently associating (1) similar past events; (2) similar absent objects; evaluating objects in terms of each other and of processes in which they are involved; and introducing imaginary objects into the play.

Tenor: Small child and parent interacting: child determining course of action, (1) announcing own intentions; (2) controlling actions of parent; concurrently sharing and seeking corroboration of own experience by verbal interaction with parent.

Mode: Spoken, alternately monologue and dialogue, task-oriented; pragmatic, (1) referring to processes and objects in the situation; (2) relating to and furthering child's own actions; (3) demanding other objects; interspersed with narrative and exploratory elements.

Field of discourse of a text

What semantic features of the text can we explain by reference to features of the situation?

types of process

1. Firstly, the manipulation of objects is clearly expressed in the language through the types of process that are being talked about, which

30

are all processes of either existence and possession, or movement and location.

Processes to do with existence and possession are involved when Nigel is talking about giving and having and finding and being. Processes to do with movement and location are those where he talks about sending and carrying, or going and putting.

2. Secondly, we have in the text the particular grammatical structures associated with these process types, determining the participants that are involved in them. Thus there are structures involving two participants, one person and one object, for example when Nigel moves the train, or the father gives the train to him.

3. Thirdly, there are particular names of objects involved in the context of situation. These include, for example, things like train and engine and lorry, and accompanying features including the identifying terms *blue* and *black*, pieces of furniture, the chair, the floor, the railway line, and so on.

4. Fourthly, there are past events recalled by Nigel as he plays. Hence, there is a system of time reference, so that both past time and present time are involved.

5. Finally, Nigel is also evaluating the objects, as good or suitable or efficient, and so we have expressions such as *it will go* and *go well*.

All of these choices in the linguistic system belong to what we have called the experiential component, those meanings that express our experience of the world around us and inside us; and these reflect the field, the content in the sense of what is going on at the time. The child is playing with his toys and sharing the experience with someone else.

The experiential systems in Text 3.1 are shown diagrammatically in Figure 3.1.

Tenor of discourse of a text

If we consider the tenor, the personal relationships involved, we see a similar type of systematic relationship between the categories of the situation on the one hand and those of the text on the other.

1. Firstly, the interaction between parent and child is most directly expressed in terms of the person selections in the grammar. In this particular child's grammar, at this age, he refers to himself as *you* and to his father as *Daddy*; so the two personal forms are *you*, meaning 'me', and *Daddy*.

2. Secondly, Nigel is determining the course of action—he is the one who is carrying the play forward; and this is expressed through the choice of mood, again of course in terms of the child's grammar at the time. He has statements and questions on the one hand, and demands on the other. choice of mood

As far as the demands are concerned, the child announces his own intentions, and these are expressed through his current version of the first-person imperative, namely *you want to*, which means 'I want to'; but he is also controlling the actions of the parent, and this is

Figure 3.1 Experiential systems in Text 3.1

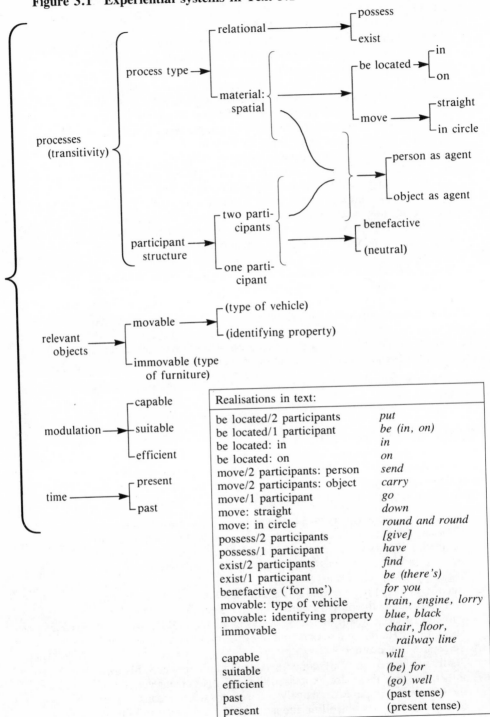

expressed through the other form of the imperative, namely *want Daddy to*, which is the form addressed to the second person meaning 'I want you to'.

As for the statements and questions, the child is sharing his experience with the parent; that is to say, he is verbalising his own experience of the play and using this as a means of checking, saying what he is doing so that the parent has the chance of agreeing or else contradicting if he thinks this is not an appropriate way of representing what is going on. Hence there are the statement and question forms in the dialogue with the function of asking and agreeing and contradicting.

Thus the systems of mood and person, which are interpersonal systems in the language, reflect very closely the father–child relationship and the form that the interaction is taking between them. These are shown diagrammatically in Figure 3.2.

Figure 3.2   Interpersonal systems in Text 3.1

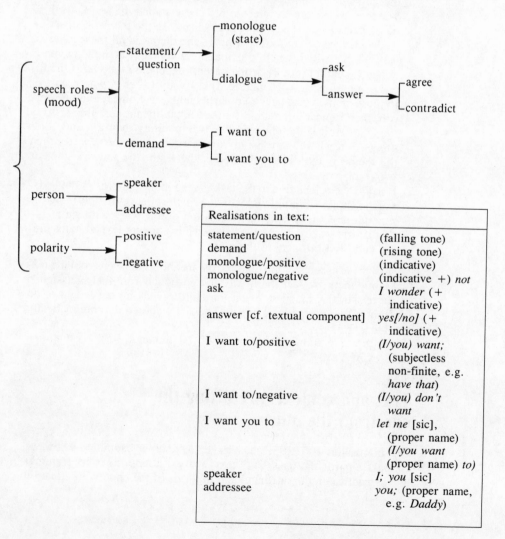

Realisations in text:	
statement/question	(falling tone)
demand	(rising tone)
monologue/positive	(indicative)
monologue/negative	(indicative +) *not*
ask	*I wonder* (+ indicative)
answer [cf. textual component]	*yes[/no]* (+ indicative)
I want to/positive	*(I/you) want;* (subjectless non-finite, e.g. *have that*)
I want to/negative	*(I/you) don't want*
I want you to	*let me* [sic], (proper name) *(I/you want* (proper name) *to)*
speaker	*I; you* [sic]
addressee	*you;* (proper name, e.g. *Daddy*)

33

Mode of discourse of a text

The mode is, of course, spoken language, spontaneous speech alternating between monologue and dialogue. It is strongly pragmatic and task oriented. That is, it is related very closely to the task in hand, the actual manipulation of the objects, passing them to one another, and so forth.

1. The fact that this is dialogue is reflected clearly in the elliptical forms, the question-and-answer sequences involving ellipsis of one kind or another, like *Which engine? The little black engine?—Yes.*

2. The fact that the language is pragmatic and task oriented is reflected in the exophoric use of pronouns like *it* and *that* referring to the objects in the situation, in particular the trains.

   Exophoric items refer to items outside the text.

3. The ongoing connectedness of the monologue is expressed through the patterns of anaphoric reference, pronouns referring back to items within the text, and also through occasional conjunctions linking one process to another, in this case the child's use of *but*.

4. The theme structure is interesting. The way that the text is furthering the actions of the child is seen clearly in the thematic structure of the clauses; if we look at what is the theme in all these clauses, we find that when the child is making a demand, then the theme is either the child himself, or the parent, depending on who is the focus of the imperative, whether it is 'I want to' or 'I want you to'. In those clauses that have two participants, one object and one person, then typically the child himself is the theme; and this reflects the fact that it is the child who is manipulating the train and other things. But where there is only one participant in the process, then the theme is the object: the lorry, the train, the railway line, or whatever it is.

   theme

5. Finally, the orientation to the task is seen in the patterns of the lexis: not the choice of individual words (which reflects the field), but the repetition of words and the collocation of one word with another—that is, the way in which the relationships among lexical items create cohesion throughout the text.

All these aspects of the texture, the meanings derived from the textual component, reflect the mode, the particular role that is assigned to the text in the situation: what the child is making the language do for him in that particular context. These are shown diagrammatically in Figure 3.3.

Figure 3.4 shows the relation of the semantic to the situational features of Text 3.1.

Text and context: predicting the one from the other

Our discussion of Text 3.1 has served as another example of how we can take a particular passage of text, analyse it in terms of its grammar and semantics on the one hand and in terms of the context of situation

Figure 3.3 Textual systems in Text 3.1

Systems:

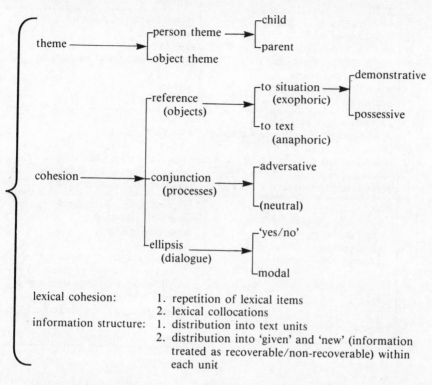

lexical cohesion:	1. repetition of lexical items
	2. lexical collocations
information structure:	1. distribution into text units
	2. distribution into 'given' and 'new' (information treated as recoverable/non-recoverable) within each unit

Realisations in text:	
person theme: child	*I/you* (initial): subjectless (non-finite)
person theme: parent	(proper name initial)
object theme	(object name initial)
exophoric: demonstrative	*this, that, the, here*
exophoric: possessive	*your* ('my')
anaphoric	*it, that, the*
adversative	*but*; (fall-rise tone)
ellipsis: 'yes/no'	*yes/no*
ellipsis: modal	(modal element, e.g. *it is, it will*)
lexical: repetition of items	(e.g. *train . . . train*)
lexical: collocations	(e.g. *chair . . . floor; train . . . railway line*)
information structure: text units	(organisation in tone groups)
information structure: given-new	(location of tonic nucleus)

on the other, and then see how the two relate together. It is this correlation between the features of the text and the features of the situation that justifies our analysis of the situation in terms of these concepts of field, tenor, and mode. We use this theoretical model because it helps

Figure 3.4 Relation of semantic to situational features in Text 3.1

	Situational	Semantic
Field	manipulation of objects assistance of adult movable objects and fixtures movability of objects and their relation to fixtures recall of similar events evaluation	process type and participant structure benefactive type of relevant object type of location and movement past time modulation
Tenor	interaction with parent determination of course of action enunciation of intention control of action sharing of experience seeking corroboration of experience	person mood and polarity demand, 'I want to' demand, 'I want you to' statement/question, monologue statement/question, dialogue

Mode	dialogue
	reference to situation
	textual cohesion: objects
	textual cohesion: processes
	furthering child's actions
	
	orientation to task
	spoken mode
		ellipsis (question-answer)
		exophoric reference
		anaphoric reference
		conjunction
		theme (in conjunction with transitivity
		  and mood; typically, parent or
		  child in demands, child in two-
		  participant statements, object in
		  one-participant statements)
		lexical collocation and repetition
		information structure

us to interpret the features that we actually find in the text. This is simply our way of explaining what the members of the culture, the participants in any given context of situation, actually do themselves.

The participants in a culture make use of this close relationship between the text and the situation as a basis for their own interaction. I have used the term 'prediction' to refer to this, and it is perhaps important to make one point clear. I am not saying, of course, that either the participant in the situation, or the linguist looking over his or her shoulder, can predict the text in the sense of actually guessing in advance exactly what is going to be said or written; obviously not. What I am saying is that we can and do (and must) make inferences from the situation to the text, about the kinds of meaning that are likely to be exchanged; and also inferences from the text to the situation. In the normal course of life, all day and every day, when we are interacting with others through language, we are making these inferences in both directions. We are making inferences from the situation to the text, and from the text to the situation.

There are instances where we have only one or the other to go on; and then, of course, we have to make inferences in one direction only. So there are certain kinds of text—literary text is an obvious example— in which there is no situation except the external situation of ourselves as readers, and we have to construct the inner situation entirely from our reading of the text. On the other hand, there are instances where we find ourselves for some reason or another as if we were dropped from Mars into the middle of some ongoing situation; we simply have to do a quick survey of what is happening, and this enables us to zero in on the meanings and to make predictions about what is likely to be said.

Let me give some brief examples that will show what I mean by inferring the situation from the text. If you are a speaker of English, then from these short passages you will be able to make certain inferences about the context of situation in which each might have occurred:

- If you come across *once upon a time*, then you know immediately that you are being told a traditional story, probably a children's story. There is no other context in which that expression is used. You can therefore predict quite a lot not only about what is going to follow, but also about the situation in which that is actually being used; typically, let us say, someone reading out a story to a small child.

- If you see *this is to certify that* (you only see that in writing, you never hear it), it always means that some impersonal letter is being started, usually a letter that is going to certify that some individual holds certain qualifications or has performed certain actions.

- If you hear *four hearts*, it is probably not something taken from a teenage romance novel, but a bid in a game of bridge: it can only occur at certain points in a certain card game.

- If you hear *on your marks*, then you know that it is a sports occasion at a school, probably a primary school, and that a race is about to begin; the teacher starting the race is saying *on your marks, get set, go*.

- If you hear *30 please*, it could be in a shop, but it is more likely to be on some form of public transport where the cost of the ticket is 30c; the meaning is 'I want one 30c ticket, please'.

- If you hear *just a trim, is it?*, that can only be at the men's barber's shop, where the barber, hoping perhaps that he is not going to have to work too hard, starts off by asking you if all you want is a trim.

- *Rail strike threat averted*: that can only be a newspaper headline. It would never be spoken, even in a broadcast news bulletin; it has the special grammar that is typical of headlines.

- If you hear *348-1929*, that is likely to be the announcement of a telephone number; there are not many other contexts in which you string out a lot of numbers like that.

- *Sea slight on a low swell*: this comes from a weather report, and you can not only tell that but you can also say something about what part of the world it probably comes from, because it is likely to be a weather report in some area where people do a lot of sailing and need to be informed what the conditions for sailing are like in the open sea.

- *Hands up all those who've finished* is likely to be in a primary school classroom, where children are asked to put their hands up to give a signal that they have something to say, or have done whatever was expected of them.

We are getting away from fixed phrases, into more open-ended examples; but the context is still clear. For example, *add the eggs one at a time, beating well in between* — that can only come from a cookery recipe; there is no other plausible context for it. *From here, a short walk takes you to the fountain*— that can only be from a tourist guide. There is no other place that you will find that kind of grammar.

You will notice that it is not just the content, the experiential meaning alone, that indicates the provenance of the text. One has to take account of everything in it: the particular structures that are used; the forms of the sentences, and whether they are elliptical or not; what relationships there are between the words, and so on. *Body relaxed, arms swinging from the shoulders*—that comes from the health manual in which you are told how to perform your daily exercises. Here is one that I do not understand at all—yet I could tell what kind of source it comes from, even though I have no idea what it means: *Remove battery holding down bolts, or hook bolts at both ends of battery*. This must come from an instruction manual issued to somebody who is installing or assembling appliances of some kind. No doubt he or she would know enough to understand it, which I do not.

I have given short and rather clearcut examples, but they are not untypical: a great deal of our verbal interaction does involve clearly defined speech events of this kind. We are frequently involved in uses of language in which we only need half a dozen words and we can tell immediately what the context of situation is. If I cite longer passages, then we will be able to include not only specific uses of language like these but everyday discourse as well.

For example, you might hear something like this: 'Well, I've come to see you because I've been having this pain. Had it on and off for ever such a long time and never done anything about it. Tried to forget about it, really, I suppose'. That will probably be a middle-aged or elderly woman describing her symptoms to the doctor. It is a woman's language rather than a man's language. It is an old person's language rather than a young person's. It is in a private doctor's clinic rather than a hospital; and so on. We can reconstruct a lot about the situation just by attending to that little bit of text.

Any piece of text, long or short, spoken or written, will carry with it indications of its context. We only have to hear or read a section of it to know where it comes from. This means that we reconstruct from the text certain aspects of the situation, certain features of the field, the tenor, and the mode. Given the text, we construct the situation from it.

The concept of 'register'

In order to incorporate this into our general theory, we need the concept of a variety of language, corresponding to a variety of situation: a concept of the kind of variation in language that goes with variation in the context of situation. This therefore is the point at which we need to bring in the notion of a REGISTER.

Register is a semantic concept.

A register is a semantic concept. It can be defined as a configuration of meanings that are typically associated with a particular situational configuration of field, mode, and tenor. But since it is a configuration of meanings, a register must also, of course, include the expressions, the lexico-grammatical and phonological features, that typically accompany or REALISE these meanings. And sometimes we find that a particular register also has indexical features, indices in the form of particular words, particular grammatical signals, or even sometimes phonological signals that have the function of indicating to the participants that this is the register in question, like my first example *once upon a time*. 'Once upon a time' is an indexical feature that serves to signal the fact that we are now embarking on a traditional tale.

Variations in kinds of register

The category of register will vary, from something that is closed and limited to something that is relatively free and open-ended. That is to say, there are certain registers in which the total number of possible meanings is fixed and finite and may be quite small; whereas in others, the range of the discourse is much less constrained.

Closed registers

One example of a register in which the number of meanings was small was that which was familiar to those who were in the armed services during the Second World War. The set of messages that one was allowed to send home from active service by cable was strictly controlled, and the number was very limited, somewhere around a hundred, though you could combine two or three together and say things like 'Happy birthday and please send DDT'. Since the total number of messages was limited, there was no need for the message itself to be transmitted; the only thing that was transmitted was a number. That particular message might be transmitted as '31, 67' or something of that kind. It is a characteristic of a closed register, one in which the total number of possible messages is fixed and finite, that it is not necessary to send the message; all you need to transmit is an index number.

That kind of register is, of course, an extreme case; we could refer to it by the term introduced by Firth as a RESTRICTED LANGUAGE. It is a kind of register in which there is no scope for individuality, or for creativity. The range of possible meanings is fixed. Most registers are not like that; but there are some that we meet with in daily life that are near that end of the scale. For example, consider the International Language of the Air, which air crew have to learn in order to act as pilots and navigators on the international air routes today. They have to communicate with ground control, they have to used a fixed language in which to do so, and they have to keep the total messages within a certain range. They will not start discussing the latest fashions, or anything of that kind.

Many of the languages of games are of this restricted nature, like the bidding system in bridge that I referred to earlier. There are only a certain number of possible messages, like 'four hearts'. Of course, you can start chatting about other things in the middle of the game;

restricted registers

but then you are going outside the register. The register itself is restricted. Some such registers are interesting because they actually have a special language, which reflects their origins in the culture: in the West, for example, the register of musical scores is Italian, because Italian was the language through which musical culture spread around Europe in the fifteenth century. The language of menus, which is also a fairly restricted register, has traditionally been French.

More open registers

Coming to somewhat more open varieties, we can recognise the language of minor documents like tickets, and of official forms. Then in English-speaking countries we have a special register for verses on greeting cards, which are sent to people on their birthdays or other personal occasions. They are probably written by computer. Rather more open than these are the registers of headlines, and of recipes; still more open-ended, the registers of technical instructions, and of legal documents. Then there are the various transactional registers, like those of buying and selling at an auction, in a shop, or in a market; and the register of communication between doctor and patient.

There are styles of meaning associated with these registers, which simply have to be learnt. Medical students coming from overseas to English-speaking countries generally learn the technical language quite easily; but when it comes to having to communicate with the patients, they often have a great deal of difficulty, because this is a very different register, and one that is not taught in the textbooks. It is now being specially studied, with a view to helping foreign students to learn it.

Another register, or set of registers, to which a lot of attention is now being paid is the language of the classroom: the language used between teacher and pupils in primary and secondary schools. There is often quite some difference between these two levels in English-speaking countries, and one of the things that children find most difficult about the transition from primary school to secondary school is the need to learn a new set of registers, embodying a new pattern of relationship between teacher and taught.

We are now approaching the other end of the register scale. Consider our various kinds of conversational strategies, the forms of discourse that we use in everyday interaction with other people when we are trying to persuade them or entertain them or teach them or whatever it is we want to do. These are the most open-ended kind of register, the registers of informal narrative and spontaneous conversation. Yet

even these are never totally open-ended. There is no situation in which the meanings are not to a certain extent prescribed for us. There is always some feature of which we can say, 'This is typically associated with this or that use of language'. Even the most informal spontaneous conversation has its strategies and styles of meaning. We are never selecting with complete freedom from all the resources of our linguistic system. If we were, there would be no communication; we understand each other only because we are able to make predictions, subconscious guesses, about what the other person is going to say.

Registers and dialects

Registers and dialects are two sorts of variety of a language.

A dialect, or dialectal variety, can be defined as a variety of language according to the user. That is, the dialect is what you speak habitually, depending in principle on who you are; and that means where you come from, either geographically in the case of regional dialects, or socially in the case of social dialects. In modern urban life, of course, the dialect pattern is predominantly a social one, so that dialect variation reflects the social order, in the particular sense of the social structure.

A register we can define as a variety according to use. In other words, the register is what you are speaking at the time, depending on what you are doing and the nature of the activity in which the language is functioning. So whereas, in principle at least, any individual might go through life speaking only one dialect (in modern complex societies this is increasingly unlikely; but it is theoretically possible, and it used to be the norm), it is not possible to go through life using only one register. The register reflects another aspect of the social order, that of social processes, the different types of social activity that people commonly engage in.

Hence, in principle, dialects are saying the same thing in different ways, whereas registers are saying different things. So dialects tend to differ not in the meanings they express but in the realisations of these meanings at other levels—in their grammar, in their vocabulary, in their phonology, in their phonetics. On the other hand it is precisely in their meanings that registers are differentiated from each other. Of course they must also differ in grammar and in vocabulary, because grammar and vocabulary are what express the meanings; but this is simply a consequence of the difference in semantic potential. Registers do not usually differ in phonology, although some registers do acquire distinctive voice qualities.

The extreme cases of dialectal differentiation are phenomena like anti-languages (dialects of criminal or other opposed subcultures) and anti-languages mother-in-law languages (dialects for addressing those in a counterposed kinship relation). Such dialectal varieties have a special function in a culture, reflecting some sharp division within the social structure. Extreme cases of register differentiation are those I have been referring to as 'restricted languages', registers that have developed for some special purpose, which itself is narrowly restricted. These are the extreme cases.

Most of the time in everyday life we meet with intermediate cases. In dialects, we meet with subcultural varieties, dialects that reflect castes or social classes, or the distinction between town and country, or between parents and children, old and young, male and female, and so on. On the register side, the intermediate varieties are those technical and institutional registers such as doctor—patient communication, classroom discourse, and the like. These are less closed than weather reports and recipes, but less open than informal discussions among friends and colleagues.

The concepts of dialect and register are mutually defining, so that a functional relationship exists between the two. Registers are the semantic configurations that are typically associated with particular social contexts, defined as we have defined them in terms of field, tenor, and mode. They vary from, at one end, the kind of action-oriented registers in which there is a lot of activity and little talk, sometimes referred to under the name of 'language in action', to the talk-oriented registers in which most of the activity is linguistic and there is not much else going on.

But there is, also, a close interconnection in practice between registers and dialects. There is a division of labour in society: different social groups, speaking different dialects, engage in different kinds of activity. As a consequence of this, certain registers come to be associated with certain dialects. In a typical Western society, if you are using the bureaucratic register you switch on the standard dialect, no matter what dialect you speak at other times. And, on the other hand, different social groups often tend to have different conceptions of the meanings that are appropriate to given contexts of situation—that is, they have what Bernstein (1971) refers to as different coding orientations. So there are various lines of interconnection between dialect and register; but conceptually the two are distinct. See Table 3.1 for a summary of the differences between dialect and register.

When we face a particular text, in order to interpret it in relation to its context, we assign it to some register. We see it as an instance of that particular functional variety. Clearly, from one point of view, every text is different from every other text. Even if the same words have been spoken or written thousands and millions of times before, each instance is in a certain sense unique. Some texts are truly unique and are indeed highly valued for their uniqueness; it is this property we have in mind when we say that something belongs to the rather vaguely defined category of 'literature'. A literary text is a text that is valued in its own right, which must mean that it differs from all other texts.

literary texts

But at the same time it is also true that every text is in some sense like other texts; and for any given text there will be some that it resembles more closely. There are classes of texts, and this is what gives us the general notion of a register. The feeling we have, as speakers of language, that this text is like that one is simply a recognition that they belong in some respect to the same register.

Table 3.1 Varieties in language

Dialects ('dialectal varieties')	Registers ('diatypic varieties')
Variety 'according to user': dialect is 'what you speak (habitually)' i.e. determined by who you are geographically or socially (region &/or social class of origin &/or adoption)	Variety 'according to use': register is 'what you are speaking (at the time)' i.e. determined by what you are doing (nature of activity in which language is functioning)
dialect reflects social order in sense of social *structure* (types of social hierarchy)	register reflects social order in sense of social *process* (types of social activity)
Hence in principle dialects are *saying the same thing differently*	Hence in principle registers are *saying different things*
So dialects tend to differ in:	So registers tend to differ in:
phonetics phonology vocabulary grammar (to a certain extent) but not in semantics	semantics and *therefore* in grammar & vocabulary (as expression of meanings) but rarely in phonology (some require special voice qualities)
The extreme case of dialectal differentiation is:	The extreme case of register differentiation is:
'anti-languages' 'mother-in-law languages'	restricted languages languages for special purposes
Intermediate cases are:	Intermediate cases are:
subcultural varieties	occupational varieties
caste or social class provenance (rural/urban) generation (parents/children) age (old/young) sex (male/female)	technical (scientific, technological) institutional (e.g. doctor—patient) other contexts having special structures & strategies (e.g. classroom)
Note: Members of a community often hold strong attitudes towards its dialects, owing to the function of dialect in the expression and maintenance of social hierarchy. One dialect may acquire special status as symbolising the values of the community as a whole.	Note: Registers are the semantic configurations that are typically associated with particular social contexts (defined in terms of field, tenor, and mode). They may vary from 'action-oriented' (much action, little talk) to 'talk-oriented' (much talk, little action).

BUT there is close interconnection between registers and dialects; so there is no very sharp line between the two. There is 'division of labour': different members have different social roles — so certain registers demand certain dialects (e.g. bureaucratic register: standard dialect), and on the other hand different social groups may tend to have different conceptions of the meanings that are exchanged in particular situations (Bernstein's 'codes').

Coda

Text, context, and learning

Text as a metafunctional construct

We study language partly in order to understand language and how it works, and partly in order to understand what people do with it. The two questions are closely connected: the way language is organised has been determined, over the million and more years of its evolution, by the functions it is called on to serve. Like any other tool, it is shaped by its purposes. A 'functional' theory of language is a theory that brings this out.

From a very early age, before even the human child has started learning the 'mother tongue', he—we will call it 'he'—discovers that he can engage in acts of meaning. He can understand symbols that are addressed to him, and he can construct symbols that those around him will understand. Typically, by the time he is one year old, a baby has mastered the principle of such acts of meaning: that they have two basic functions—for doing, and for learning. Like the office memorandum, language is either 'for action' or 'for information'.

You address a symbol to someone, by gesture, or by voice, either because you want them to do something for you—play with you, perhaps, or hand you something out of your reach; or because you are learning about the world and your place in it—noting what interests you and what you recognise as familiar, and sharing your experiences with them. And this dual motif becomes the prime strategy for mastering the mother tongue, the language of the adult world.

These are the two ways of meaning that lie behind the various functional approaches to language that we described in Chapter 2. They are the so-called METAFUNCTIONS of systemic theory, which we refer to as INTERPERSONAL and IDEATIONAL. (The term 'experiential', used in the descriptions, is simply the ideational metafunction minus the abstract logical component.) The interpersonal is the doing function; the ideational is the learning or thinking function. But these are not simply more fancy names for the same things. The meaning of metafunction is 'that part of the system of a language—the particular semantic and lexico-grammatical resources—that has evolved to perform the function in question'. As we saw throughout Chapter 2, in English (as ther language), each of these metafunctions makes a clear a   ative contribution to the grammar. But it does so in a way th   different from the 'either/or' of the functional theories from ou   anguistics, according to which each utterance is **either** this **or** that (either transactional or poetic etc.). This sort of exclusive alternation is true in an infant's protolanguage, where each symbol is doing only one thing. But it is not true of an adult language. Adult languages are organised in such a way that every utterance is **both** this **and** that: has both an interpersonal and ideational component to it. It does something, and it is about something. This is the basis of the 'metafunction' theory.

We also noted that there is a third metafunctional component in language to which there is no corresponding function in the sense of 'use'—it is not a way of using language, but rather a resource for ensuring that what is said is relevant and relates to its context. This we refer to as the TEXTUAL metafunction.

To be able to read a text, or listen to it, effectively and with understanding, we have to be able to interpret it in terms of all these metafunctions. In other words, anyone who is learning by listening to a teacher, or reading a textbook, has to:

1a. understand the processes being referred to, the participants in these processes, and the circumstances—time, cause, etc.—associated with them [EXPERIENTIAL];
1b. understand the relationship between one process and another, or one participant and another, that share the same position in the text [LOGICAL];
2. recognise the speech function, the type of offer, command, statement, or question, the attutudes and judgments embodied in it, and the rhetorical features that constitute it as a symbolic act [INTERPERSONAL]; and
3. grasp the news value and topicality of the message, and the coherence between one part of the text and every other part [TEXTUAL].

By understanding the functional organisation of language, we are enabled to explain success and failure in learning through language: where a breakdown occurs, why it occurs, and how to overcome it and prevent it from occurring again. We can also see how far the fault lies in the learner and how far it lies in the language that is being used to teach him or her.

Context of situation

All use of language has a context. The 'textual' features enable the discourse to cohere not only with itself but also with its context of situation. We have analysed the context of situation into three components, corresponding to the three metafunctions. This enables us to display the redundancy between text and situation—how each serves to predict the other. The three components are:

1. field of discourse: the 'play'—the kind of activity, as recognised in the culture, within which the language is playing some part [predicts experiential meanings];

2. tenor of discourse: the 'players'—the actors, or rather the intering roles, that are involved in the creation of the text [predicts
   interpersonal meanings]; and
3. mode of discourse: the 'parts'—the particular functions that are
   assigned to language in this situation, and the rhetorical channel that
   is therefore allotted to it [predicts textual meanings].

The context of situation, as defined in these terms, is the immediate
environment in which a text is actually functioning. We use this notion
to explain why certain things have been said or written on this particular occasion, and what else might have been said or written that was not.

The reason for doing this, however, is not only retrospective but
prospective. Because of the close link between text and context, readers
and listeners make predictions; they read and listen, with expectations
for what is coming next. When someone is reading or listening in order
to learn, the ability to predict in this way takes on a particular importance, as without it the whole process is slowed down. The whole point
of a passage may be missed if the reader or listener does not bring to
it appropriate assumptions derived from the context of situation.

Context of culture

Much of the work of learning a foreign language consists in learning
to make the right predictions. If the student coming into school with
a first language other than English finds difficulty in using English to
learn with, this is likely to be in part because he has not yet learnt to
expect in English—to use the context in this predictive way.

The context of situation, however, is only the immediate environment. There is also a broader background against which the text has
to be interpreted: its CONTEXT OF CULTURE. Any actual context of situation, the particular configuration of field, tenor, and mode that has
brought a text into being, is not just a random jumble of features but
a totality—a package, so to speak, of things that typically go together
in the culture. People do these things on these occasions and attach
these meanings and values to them; this is what a culture is.

The school itself provides a good example of what in modern jargon could be called an 'interface' between the context of situation and
the context of culture. For any 'text' in school—teacher talk in the classroom, pupil's notes or essay, passage from a textbook—there is always
a context of situation: the lesson, with its concept of what is to be
achieved; the relationship of teacher to pupil, or textbook writer to reader;
the 'mode' of question-and-answer, expository writing, and so on. But
these in turn are instances of, and derive their meaning from, the school
as an institution in the culture: the concept of education, and of educational knowledge as distinct from commonsense knowledge; the notion
of the curriculum and of school 'subjects'; the complex role structures
of teaching staff, school principals, consultants, inspectorate, departments of education, and the like; and the unspoken assumptions about
learning and the place of language within it.

All these factors constitute the context of culture, and they determine, collectively, the way the text is interpreted in its context of situation. It is as well to know what we are assuming, as teachers, when we stand up in front of a class and talk, or when we set pupils a task like writing a report or an essay, or when we evaluate their performance in that task.

We have not offered, here, a separate linguistic model of the context of culture; no such thing yet exists, although there are useful ideas around. But in describing the context of situation, it is helpful to build in some indication of the cultural background, and the assumptions that have to be made if the text is to be interpreted—or produced—in the way the teacher (or the system) intends.

Intertextuality

The context of situation and the wider context of culture make up the non-verbal environment of a text. We have spoken of these as 'determining' the text, stressing the predictability of the text from the context; and this is an important perspective, since it helps us to understand how people actually exchange meanings and interact with one another. But in fact the relationship between text and context is a dialectical one: the text creates the context as much as the context creates the text. 'Meaning' arises from the friction between the two. This means that part of the enviroment for any text is a set of previous texts, texts that are taken for granted as shared among those taking part. Again, the school provides very clear examples. Every lesson is built on the assumption of earlier lessons in which topics have been explored, concepts agreed upon and defined; but beyond this there is a great deal of unspoken cross-reference of which everyone is largely unaware.

This kind of INTERTEXTUALITY, as it is sometimes called, includes not only the more obviously experiential features that make up the context of a lesson but also other aspects of the meaning: types of logical sequencing that are recognised as valid, even interpersonal features such as whether a question is intended to be answered or is being used as a step in the development of an argument. There are also likely to be 'coded' expressions that are carried on from one text to another, more or less fomulaic sequences that may signal what is happening, or what is going to happen next. That is why it is so difficult to come in the middle of an ongoing discourse of this kind, such as joining in a new class half-way through the school year. The problem can be eased if the 'intertextual' assumptions can be made explicit—perhaps as a function of pupil solidarity, as when a newcomer is told 'When Mr Smith says "Well if there are no more questions", it means he's going to quiz us on what he's just been saying'.

At a deeper level the entire school learning experience is linked by a pervading 'intertextuality' that embodies the theory and practice of education as institutionalised in our culture. There is a sense in which the classroom is one long text, that carries over from one year to the next and from one stage of schooling to the next. Unfortunately most studies of educational discourse have tended to concentrate on the mechanics of classroom interaction. Other study units in this program are attempting to get at more fundamental aspects of the linguistic processes by which school pupils learn.

Coherence

Finally we come back to the text itself; but at one level up, so to speak. Every text is also a context for itself. A text is characterised by coherence; it hangs together. At any point after the beginning, what has gone before provides the enviroment for what is coming next. This sets up internal expectations; and these are matched up with the expectations referred to earlier, that the listener or reader brings from the external sources, from the context of situation and of culture.

An important contribution to coherence comes from COHESION: the set of linguistic resources that every language has (as part of the textual metafunction) for linking one part of a text to another. In Chapter 5 below we shall be discussing these resources as they appear in English, under the headings of (1) REFERENCE, (2) SUBSTITUTION and ELLIPSIS, (3) CONJUNCTION, and (4) LEXICAL COHESION. These are the semantic relations that enable one part of the text to function as the context for another.

A teacher is often called on to judge the coherence of a text. Most typically, perhaps, when evaluating the pupils' writing; and very often all the pupil is told is 'this doesn't hang together'—when what he needs to know is why it doesn't hang together, and how it could be made to do so. Without an understanding of the linguistic resources involved it is impossible to give the explicit help that is needed.

But there are other occasions besides. There are many instances where it is the textbook that doesn't hang together; and a critical linguistic analysis of a difficult passage of a classroom text can be extraordinarily revealing when the teacher is trying to find out where the students' problems arise. Every sentence may be impeccable in itself; but if the preceding sequence of sentences does not provide a context with which what follows can cohere then the effect will be one of confusion: not simply 'I can't understand this', but 'I can't understand what it is I can't understand'.

Every part of a text, therefore, is at once both text and context. In focusing attention on the language with which people learn, we should be aware of both these functions. Each element in the discourse, whether just one phrase or an entire chapter or a book, has a value (1) as text, in itself, and (2) as context, to other text that is to come. A functional grammar enables us to take both these into account.

Text, context, and learning

We have identified five periods in the cycle of text and context:

1. the text, as a metafunctional construct: a complex of ideational, interpersonal, and textual meanings;

2. the context of situation: the configuration of field, tenor, and mode features that specify the register of the text;
3. the context of culture: the institutional and ideological background that give value to the text and constrain its interpretation;
4. the 'intertextual' context: relations with other texts, and assumptions that are carried over therefrom;
5. the 'intratextual' context: coherence within the text, including the linguistic cohesion that embodies the internal semantic relationships.

All learning is a process of contextualisation: a building up of expectancies about what will happen next. These include non-verbal expectancies: if I wire this in here, that switch will operate there. But most learning takes place through language, especially learning in school; and the linguistic expectancies are critical to its success.

To succeed in mathematics, for example, I need to understand the sentence:

> Every regular polygon has rotational symmetry about a certain point called its **centre** for various angles of rotation.

To be able to understand it, I have to have a context for it. Into this context come elements from all five periods listed above. It would take a longish chapter to write them all out, and I shall not attempt to do so here. But only a very small part of the demands made by that sentence lies in understanding its technical terms. We need to bring to it a considerable resource drawn from (1) the metafunctional systems of modern English, (2) praxis in the study of mathematics, (3) accepted patterns of reasoning in the culture, (4) other mathematical texts, and (5) the surrounding matter, such as figures, in the text itself—and to be able to see its relationship to all of these.

We tend to think of learning exclusively as a cognitive process, and to neglect its linguistic aspects. What we are attempting to do here is to interpret learning as a linguistic process, taking some tentative steps towards a linguistic theory of learning that would complement the established cognitive models. This should enable teachers and others concerned to explore the value and critical role of language in education and to appreciate how deeply children depend on language in order to be able to learn.

Part B
Ruqaiya Hasan

Chapter 4

The structure of a text

Introduction

Let me begin from one of the basic questions that Halliday has already raised in Chapter 1: what is text? My aim is to elaborate upon the definition he has offered: 'we can define text in the simplest way . . . as language that is functional. By functional, we simply mean language that is doing some job in some context . . .'. I want to show in some detail what it means to define text, as Halliday does, as 'language that is functional', 'that is doing some job in some context of situation'. My main hypothesis will be that text and context are so intimately related that neither concept can be enunciated without the other.

See p. 10.

But before broaching this main topic, let me begin by taking the word 'text' in its rather general sense—the sense that is enshrined in *Chambers' Twentieth Century Dictionary* as:

> the actual words of a book, poem etc., in their original form or any form they have been transmitted in or transmuted into . . .

Thinking of text this way, what could one say about its most outstanding characteristics? The attribute that comes to mind most readily is that of UNITY. Clearly we can't know—in the sense of being acquainted with—all the books, poems etc., either in their original form or otherwise; but clearly, also, we do know texts—in the sense of being able to discriminate between a text and a 'non-text', a complete text and an incomplete one. I am suggesting that the basis for these judgments lies in the notion of unity.

The unity in any text—whether written as Chambers' definition implies, or spoken as face-to-face interaction requires—is of two major types:

- unity of structure
- unity of texture.

I am going to discuss the unity of structure first. Texture will be discussed in the following chapter.

What is text structure?

Structure is a familiar term, but what does it mean in the expression 'the structure of a text'? Probably the easiest way to explain it is to give a paraphrase, to say, for example, that it refers to the overall structure, the global structure of the message form. A simple example will serve to illustrate what is meant here. While I was a visitor in Japan, my colleagues took me to see a Kabuki play, and I had the need and the opportunity to learn a little about this famous art form. On reading a little booklet relating to Kabuki, I learned that there is a genre known as Sewamono within which there is a particular sub-genre known as Enkirimono. I learned also that the basic pattern in Enkirimono is that there is a breaking off of relations, either between a married couple, or between lovers. The reason for this break is not known to one of the participants, the forsaken member of the relationship, who takes it as an act of cruel desertion; but in actual fact the real motive behind the desertion is a noble one. For example, a husband might divorce a wife in order to prevent her from suffering the consequences of some crime that he might have commited. Now, on the basis of this much information, I could postulate that in every instance of Enkirimono, there will be at least three elements of structure. I will give these elements descriptive names, so that they may, hopefully, have a mnemonic value:

1. the Precipitative Event: an event that propels from one stage to another. It would thus lead to the second element. An example of a Precipitative Event, perhaps, would be the geisha rejecting her lover, or the husband informing his wife that he is divorcing her;
2. the Consequential Event: an event brought about as a consequence of the Precipitative Event;
3. the Revelation: the Consequential Event leads to some revelation of facts hitherto concealed. The Revelation leads to a re-interpretation of the Precipitative Event; the nobility of the act becomes obvious. What had appeared as heartless forsaking now assumes heroic proportions, being seen in its true colour as an act of devotion and self-sacrifice.

Structure is made up of separate events or elements.

Assuming that my understanding of Enkirimono, sketchy though it is, is nonetheless correct in essentials, we have postulated three elements that are essential to the structure of every Enkirimono text; and these are: Precipitative Event, Consequential Event, and Revelation. We can refer to literary studies for this kind of concept of text structure. The earliest widely known Western model is the Aristotelian definition of Greek tragedy as made up of three elements: the beginning, the middle, and the end. One may have reservations about this actual analysis; I am not concerned with that here. My only concern is to provide such examples as will clarify my own use of the terms 'element of text structure' and 'generic structure of text'. So, as a first step, I have referred to two genres: that of Enkirimono and that of Greek tragedy. In each case I have shown the presence of elements of structure. But drama, epic, fables, or sonnets—no matter how much valued by a community—are not particularly privileged in this respect. Even the

the Aristotelian definition of structure

structure in casual
conversation

use of language that appears most effortless and least specialised, namely casual conversation, possesses structure in this sense (Ventola, 1979).

Between classical tragedy and the everyday common phenomenon of casual conversation (Ventola, 1979), there exists a wide range of genres, varying in the extent to which the global structure of their message form appears to have a definite shape. Strange as it may sound, the structure of casual conversation is much less well understood, even by those of us who specialise in talking about conversation, than that of, say, the Petrarchan sonnet. Many of us would be surprised by the suggestion that there is structure in a text generated in the course of buying a kilo of potatoes and three cloves of garlic.

In this chapter, I propose to abandon the better described genres of literature in favour of one that is much closer to the conversation end of the spectrum. The invisibility of structure in the latter type of genres is justification enough for the decision; but there is a deeper reason. An understanding of genres from everyday situations—particularly those in which language acts as an instrument, for example in the context of canoeing from Malinowski—helps us to see clearly the very close partnership between language and the living of life.

See p. 6.

Such understanding assists in describing the relationship between language and context in those areas too where this partnership is not so obvious. This is often the case with written text, but particularly with texts of verbal art, philosophy, and science—in fact, all areas outside the domain of commonsense knowledge. To explain the relationship between texts of the latter type to their context, we must invoke Malinowski's notion of context of culture. Although I shall be discussing some aspects of this question in Chapter 6, there will not be enough time to follow up the question in as great a detail as is needed to talk about the relationship of context to text structure. Here, I will choose a genre that is closer to the canoeing situation than it is to, say, the nursery tale (Hasan, 1984) or a fable (Halliday, 1977). It is embedded in a type of context that could be described as FOCUSED INTERACTION, and, within that, more specifically it belongs to the genre of SERVICE ENCOUNTER where the participants bear the role of seeker and supplier of goods and/or services.

See pp. 99–101, and
Hasan, 'The nursery
tale as genre' (1984)
and *Linguistics,
Language and Verbal
Art* (1989).

A text and its context

Let us first introduce a text.

Text 4.1

genre: Service
Encounter

C: Can I have ten oranges and a kilo of bananas please?
V: Yes, anything else?
C: No, thanks.
V: That'll be dollar forty.
C: Two dollars.
V: Sixty, eighty, two dollars. Thank you.

Text 4.1 is an example of the genre Service Encounter. Anyone who knows the English language and is generally acquainted with the Western type of culture will have no difficulty in 'placing' this text into the context that is appropriate to it. Earlier Halliday considered the

See p. 9.

question 'how do we explain the success with which people communicate?'. If it is true, as he suggested, that 'the situation in which linguistic interaction takes place gives the participants a great deal of information about the meanings that are being exchanged, and . . . that are likely to be exchanged', then it is equally true that the meanings that are being made by the language will give the participants a great deal of information about the kind of situation they are in.

See p. 10.

I emphasise this two-way relationship between language and situation, for both theoretical and practical reasons. Theoretically, this emphasis reveals the un-commonsense view of situation. The commonsense view is that we say 'Can I have . . .', 'How much is that?', 'That'll be six dollars seventy', and so on, because we happen to be in a shopping situation. The un-commonsense view is that shopping as a culturally recognisable type of situation has been constructed over the years by the use of precisely this kind of language. Without the recognition of this bi-directionality, it would be difficult to account for the possibility of verbal art, science, philosophy—in fact, the entire domain of human knowledge—or, for that matter, deceptions and misunderstandings.

Situations are culturally constructed.

From a practical point of view, too, this emphasis is important, because as I begin to explore the details of the relationship between context and text structure, I may, in the interest of brevity, limit myself to showing how some feature of the context can be used to predict some element(s) of the structure of possible and appropriate texts. Such statements should be read as implying that, all else being equal, the presence of those elements of the text's structure would 'construct' those same features of the context. We can now turn to the question of how context affects the structure of the text.

Contextual configuration

Halliday has introduced the three terms field, tenor, and mode. These refer to certain aspects of our social situations that always act upon the language as it is being used. I should like to introduce here a related concept: CONTEXTUAL CONFIGURATION, using the acronym CC instead of the full label.

A brief gloss of these terms can be found in Chapter 1, p. 12.

Each of the three, field, tenor, and mode, may be thought of as a variable that is represented by some specific value(s). Each functions as a point of entry to any situation as a set of possibilities—or, to use a technical term, OPTIONS. Thus, the variable field may have the value 'praising' or 'blaming'; tenor may allow a choice between 'parent-to-child' or 'employer-to-employee' while mode might be 'speech' or 'writing'. Now given that any member of a related pair of options can combine with any member of any other, the following are some of the possible configurations:

Contextual configuration = CC.

- parent praising child in speech
- employer praising employee in speech
- parent blaming child in speech
- employer blaming employee in speech.

examples of contextual configurations

Each of these entries is a CC. A CC is a specific set of values that realises field, tenor, and mode.

Contextual configuration and text structure: general remarks

We need the notion of CC for talking about the structure of the text because it is the specific features of a CC—the values of the variable—that permit statements about the text's structure. We cannot work from the general notion of, say, 'field' since it is not possible to claim, for example, that field always leads to the appearance of this or that element. Moreover, often a combination of features from more than one variable might motivate the appearance of some single element of a text (Hasan, 1978). We need to see the total set of features—all the selected values of the three variables—as one configuration, rather than attempting to relate aspects of the text's structure to individual 'headings'.

In the structural unity of the text, the CC plays a central role. If text can be described as 'language doing some job in some context', then it is reasonable to describe it as the verbal expression of a social activity; the CC is an account of the significant attributes of this social activity. So, it is not surprising that the features of the CC can be used for making certain kinds of predictions about text structure. These are as follows:

CC as an account of the significant attributes of a social activity

1. **What** elements **must** occur;
2. **What** elements **can** occur;
3. **Where must** they occur;
4. **Where can** they occur;
5. **How often** can they occur.

predictions about elements of text structure

More succinctly we would say that a CC can predict the OBLIGATORY (1) and the OPTIONAL (2) elements of a text's structure as well as their SEQUENCE (3 and 4) *vis-à-vis* each other and the possibility of their ITERATION (5). These points are discussed in the following sections. Here let me say that an ELEMENT is a stage with some consequence in the progression of a text.

Text 4.1 and its context

Look again at Text 4.1. What kind of CC would such a text be embedded in (always assuming that it was created as an appropriate response to a real-life situation)? Let us examine the values of the three variables briefly.

The field of discourse for text 4.1

Field, being concerned with the nature of the social activity, involves both the kind of acts being carried out and their goal(s). Here, there is a short-term goal of acquiring some food-stuffs in exchange for some money. This is what we refer to as 'buying', and buying always implies selling.

The tenor of discourse for Text 4.1

This social activity is institutionalised. And so the nature of the activity predicates the set of roles relevant to the unfolding of the activity (Hasan, 1980). Let us refer to this as the AGENT ROLES component of the tenor

agent roles

of discourse; these are quite obviously vendor and customer. This is what the 'V' and 'C' stand for in Text 4.1.

Cutting across the agent role is another component of tenor, which is also susceptible to whether or not the activity is institutionalised. This is the component concerned with the degree of control (or power) one participant is able to exercise over the other(s), almost by virtue of their agent role relation. You will note that the agent roles construct DYADS. If the dyad is HIERARCHIC, one agent will have a greater degree of control over the other; if it is NON-HIERARCHIC, then we have relations of peer-hood, such as those of friendship, rivalry, acquaintanceship, and indifference.

For Text 4.1, the dyad is hierarchic; within the range of the social activity, the customer exercises greater power. The vendor is in a soliciting position, having to sell the goods. It is important to recognise that control may shift from one agent to the other, and that a person carrying a subordinate hierarchic role in the agent dyad is not necessarily submissive.

Both agent role and dyadic relation are essentially determined by reference to general social matters. We might even say that in as much as agent roles and their dyadic structures are determined by the nature of the social activity, these are expressions of a social structure. But tenor is also concerned with those relations between participants that arise from their biographies. It makes a good deal of difference to the job that language has to do if I buy my kilo of potatoes from a vendor whose shop I use only irregularly as opposed to one who is also my next-door neighbour. The component of tenor that relates such details of biography to the details of social structure may be referred to as SOCIAL DISTANCE (Hasan 1973, 1978, 1980).

roles determined by social matters

social distance

Social distance is a continuum, the two end-points of which may be referred to as MAXIMAL and MINIMAL. A maximal social distance obtains when the persons involved know each other through infrequent encounters only in the capacity of the agent of some one institutionalised activity and in the dyadic status that correlates with the agent role. Thus my social distance to a vendor is maximal if as a day-tourist I walk into his or her—let's say her—store to buy some fruit and I meet her for the first time, since I only know her as a vendor. This distance is likely to be less if the vendor were someone from whom I had been buying fruit over the years; it would be even less, if I also know her in some other capacity. For example the vendor and I may belong to a club, or she may be a neighbour or a relative. The more minimal the social distance, the greater the degree of familiarity between the carriers of the role. Social distance affects styles of communication. In a long-standing relationship, for example, that of marriage, one participant is normally able to predict a great deal of what the other might say or do. So the need for explicitness is not so pressing. The tenor values for Text 4.1 are perhaps quite obvious now: the social distance between the vendor and customer is near maximal.

social distance and style of communication

The mode of discourse for Text 4.1

The third variable, mode, can also be described under at least three different sub-headings. First, there is the question of the LANGUAGE ROLE—whether it is CONSTITUTIVE or ANCILLARY. These categories

Language role may be constitutive or ancillary.

57

should not be seen as sharply distinct but rather as the two end-points of a continuum. The role of language for Text 4.1 is largely ancillary, for it accompanies the activities of exchange of goods for money. In fact, the extent to which language is made explicit in Text 4.1 is governed by my desire to present an example from everyday familiar activities in such a way that you are able to understand all the significant aspects of it.

process sharing

The second factor to be considered under mode is that of PROCESS SHARING. Is the addressee able to share the process of text creation as it unfolds, or does the addressee come to the text when it is a finished product? Here again, there are degrees of process sharing from the most active—as in dialogue—to the most passive—as in a formal lecture.

channel

The degree to which process sharing can occur is closely related to CHANNEL. The term refers to the modality through which the addressee comes in contact with the speaker's messages—do the messages travel on air as sound waves, or are they apprehended as graven images, some form of writing? The first channel I will call PHONIC, the second GRAPHIC. Elsewhere (Hasan, 1978, 1979) I have referred to these as AURAL and VISUAL, respectively. However, these terms proved undesirable; first, because they are clearly addressee oriented, and secondly, because eye-contact, called VISUAL CONTACT, occurs most normally with the phonic channel. Most other linguists have used the terms SPOKEN and WRITTEN for the two modalitites, but this solution creates other problems, which will become obvious from the discussion of MEDIUM below.

When the channel is phonic, a favourable environment for active process sharing is created; so note, dialogues normally occur in this channel. Still, the potential of the channel for most active process sharing is not always actualised. So there are many occasions when a speaker may be allowed the floor for a considerable amount of time, without the addressee having the right to interrupt—for example, the speaker may be producing a talk for a professional group. However, even on such occasions when the addressee appears least active, he or she can influence the production of the text by providing feedback through extraverbal modalities, such as eye-contact, facial expression, a yawn, or body posture. So the physical presence of the addressee impinges on the textual processes in a way that the writer's own awareness of the needs of the addressee can hardly ever do: for one thing, in the phonic channel both the speaker and the addressee hear (and often see) the same thing at the same time. This is obviously not possible when the channel is graphic. This is the reason for claiming that process sharing is closely related to channel.

medium

The third important factor relevant to mode is MEDIUM, the primary distinction here being: is the medium SPOKEN or WRITTEN. Medium refers to the patterning the wordings themselves: for example, is there a greater degree of grammatical complexity or of lexical density? (For greater detail, see Halliday, 1989). Like process sharing and language role, the difference in patterning the wordings is again a matter of degree. It is important to emphasise that medium and channel are distinct phenomena, even though they are not unrelated. In fact, it is very likely that medium is a historical product of process sharing; and, in as much

graphic and phonic channel

as process sharing itself is related to channel variation, we could claim that variation in medium—spoken versus written—is a product of variation in channel—phonic versus graphic. Thus the use of the phonic channel encourages not only the expectation of active process sharing of a dialogue, but also that the medium would be the spoken one, while the use of the graphic channel goes not only with monologue, but also the written medium. And this pattern of co-occurrence, indeed, represents the unmarked situation. However, perhaps due to the increase in our ability to record messages, this pattern of normal co-occurrence certainly does not hold today, no matter what the historical antecedents might have been. Today, medium and channel may or may not be congruent: the matter is decided not so much by the nature of the channel as by the nature of the social activity and of the social relation between the participants. So if I walk into a vegetable store to buy fruit, the medium and the channel are likely to be congruent—spoken, phonic dialogue; and, similarly, if I have to apply for the funding fo a research project, medium and channel are most likely to be congruent—written, graphic monologue. But if I write a letter to a friend, this pattern of congruence will be disturbed: I shall use the graphic channel, but I shall tend to use the spoken medium, which would very likely neither be classified as a monologue nor as a dialogue. In common parlance, I shall write *as if* I were talking to my friend. The fact that one can use one channel in actual fact, but through the use of incongruent medium create an *as—if* condition indicates the complexity of the relationships between channel and medium, both of which are subservient to the choices in the field and tenor of discourse.

The contextual configuration of Text 4.1

The CC for Text 4.1 is summed up briefly in Table 4.1.

Table 4.1   CC1: the contextual configuration of Text 4.1

Field: Economic transaction: purchase of retail goods: perishable food . . .

Tenor: Agents of transaction: hierarchic: customer superordinate and vendor subordinate; social distance: near-maximum . . .

Mode: Language role: ancillary; channel: phonic; medium: spoken with visual contact . . .

The structure of Text 4.1

Obligatory elements

We can now use the summary account of the CC in Table 4.1 to examine Text 4.1. Text 4.1 is reproduced below in Table 4.2.

Table 4.2   The structure of Text 4.1

SR = →⌈ Can I have ten oranges and a kilo of bananas please?

SC = →⌈ Yes, anything else?
⌊ No thanks.

S = →⌈ That'll be dollar forty.

P = →⌈ Two dollars.

PC = →⌈ Sixty, eighty, two dollars. Thank you.

The text begins with a request for goods: *Can I have ten oranges and a kilo of bananas please.* This is the first obligatory element. Let us refer to this element as SALE REQUEST (SR). Its occurrence is predicted mainly because of the field values. The purchase of goods presupposes prior selection, and in a store with retail goods service, this selection must be made known to the vendor. This is basically what makes the element SR obligatory.

Sale Request = SR.

The normal pattern following a request is, of course, the granting or the rejecting of it; either is possible in a sale environment, too. I shall use the term SALE COMPLIANCE (SC) irrespective of whether the response is positive or negative. In Text 4.1, SC is positive: *Yes, anything else?* It is important to realise that *yes* is not meant just as a short form for 'Yes, you can have ten oranges and a kilo of bananas'; rather, it is an encouraging noise that says 'Yes, go on! ask for more things'. In other words, a positive SC is highly likely to contain an invitation for more purchases. Its prime purpose is sales promotion, not the granting of SR. The true granting of the SR is actually in the doing—the vendor does her part of SC as she completes getting the goods for the customer. The element SC is completed only when the customer has responded to the invitation, as in Table 4.2 where the customer's response to the invitation is *No, thanks.* The motivation for SC is to be found in both the field and the tenor values. Behind the invitation to buy some more lies the ideology of 'free enterprise'. And at the same time, the hierarchic status of the vendor is one that raises the expectation of her readiness to serve as long as required. Her 'Yes, anything else' or just 'Yes' or 'Anything else?' said on a rising intonation is thus a highly condensed message.

Sale Compliance = SC.

ideology as an essential element in Service Encounter

Note that if, for some reason, the remainder of Text 4.1 were not available, you would still know that (1) this is (part of) a buying-selling text and (2) it is incomplete. It is not incomplete because it is too short; there are shorter texts, for example 'No smoking'. Non-technically, the items of the text discussed so far could be seen as fulfilling the conditions of 'giving', but there is a crucial difference between 'giving' and 'selling'. In the latter case, not only does the buyer select, and is provided with the selected commodity; he or she must also be told the price, and the payment must be made, before the social process can be said to have been accomplished. The reason why just this much of Text 4.1 would not be taken as a complete text is because we do not have an appropriate indication that the process of purchase has been completed yet. Once the structure of the text indicates the completion of this activity, we would have no hesitation in considering the text complete.

An important part of selling is when the reckoning begins: the vendor must inform the customer what the exchange value of the goods is. The message associated with this function, I refer to as SALE (S). The next obligatory element is PURCHASE (P): the customer must offer the exchange value in return for ordered goods. The buying and selling activity is clinched by the vendor acknowledging receipt of payment. This takes some politeness formula, for example, 'Thanks', 'Great', and might additionally cover the business of handing over change, should this be necessary, as is the case in Text 4.1.

S = Sale.
P = Purchase.

So the obligatory elements of Text 4.1 are SR, SC, S, P, and PC in that order. This can be displayed as SR^SC^S^P^PC, with the sign ^ showing the order of the elements.

obligatory elements in Text 4.1

To appreciate the significance of the obligatory elements, let us look at a related text (Text 4.2), which contains some optional elements. We assume that the CC presented in Table 4.1 is relevant to Text 4.2 as well.

Optional elements

Let us first introduce Text 4.2 (see Table 4.3).

Table 4.3   Text 4.2

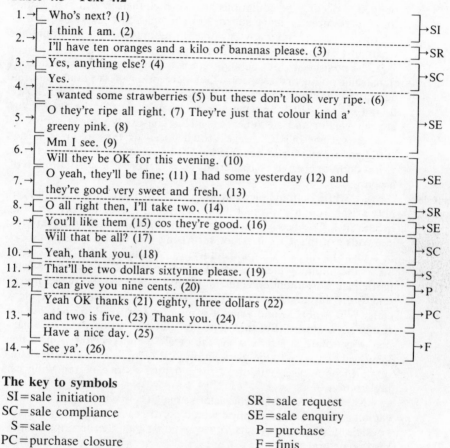

The key to symbols

SI = sale initiation	SR = sale request
SC = sale compliance	SE = sale enquiry
S = sale	P = purchase
PC = purchase closure	F = finis

In this presentation, the dotted horizontal lines show element boundaries; the initials in the right-hand column refer to the labels for structural elements; numbers within the round brackets refer to the individual messages of the text, while those in the left-hand column number the successive turns (Sacks et al., 1974) in the dialogue between the vendor and the customer.

You will note that the obligatory elements occur in Text 4.2 as well. But there are several other elements that only appear here, and not in Text 4.1. For example, the text begins with SALE INITIATION (SI), realised by messages (1) and (2). SI is an optional element. To say this is to imply that in the absence of SI, a text would still be interpreted as embedded in CC1 so long as it contains the obligatory elements. So,

optional elements in Text 4.2

61

Genre is defined by
obligatory elements in
structure.

by implication, the obligatory elements define the genre to which a text belongs; and the appearance of all of these elements in a specific order corresponds to our perception of whether the text is complete or incomplete.

So what role do optional elements have? Do they appear randomly? To say that some elements may be optional is not the same as saying 'anything goes'. The finite set of optional elements that can possibly occur in texts of the genre under focus can be stated quite definitely.

By definition, an optional element is one that **can** occur but is not obliged to occur. The conditions under which there is a high probability of its occurence can be stated. For example, SI is likely to occur in a crowded store, with many customers needing attention; it would not occur in a shop where there are no other customers.

The point is obvious enough, but note how it distinguishes the optional and obligatory elements. Our perception of the kind of social activity we are involved in does not change if the shop is crowded: we do not say this is not an economic transaction, or that the agent roles are not vendor and customer, etc. This context is viewed simply as another variant of CC1. The crowdedness of the premises is not sufficient ground for saying that the CC has changed its character; nor is it a definite enough characteristic to be criterial in the definition of a genre.

So, while optional elements do not occur randomly, their optionality arises from the fact that their occurrence is predicted by some attribute of a CC that is non-defining for the CC and to the text type embedded in that CC. It is not surprising that optional elements can be seen as having wider applicability. For example, 'Who's next?' can act as the initiating element of many other service encounters, where participant turn-initiation is institutionally controlled. So, when I go to renew my car registration, if there is a crowd, I wait till the clerk calls 'Who's next?', and when it is my turn I proceed to carry out the rest of my business. But this same procedure is not necessary if I happen to get there at a time when the office is not very busy and when I can walk right up to the clerk and say 'I'd like to renew my registration'. In both cases I think of the situation as one of renewing car registration.

Note if we wished to characterise the CCs in which such initiation can take place, the description would be so gross that we would have no idea of what specific activity was going on. The description may read something like this:

Field: Service encounter
Tenor: Institutionalised agents
Mode: Phonic channel; spoken medium.

Iterative elements

In Text 4.2, you will notice several entries marked SE. SE is an optional element and stands for SALE ENQUIRY. It can occur at any point after SI and its function is to determine some attribute of the goods contemplated for purchase. It can either be raised by the customer or the vendor and is completed when the other participant has responded, if such response is required as in (6) or (10). Note that like initiation, enquiry too could be seen as a possible feature of any service encounter. For example, in renewing my registration, I might ask the clerk 'I got married last week. Can the registration be renewed in my married name?'.

When a particular (set of) element(s) occurs more than once, we refer to this phenomenon as ITERATION, or RECURSION (Hasan, 1979). For Text 4.2, SE would be labelled an iterative (or recursive) element. As a linguistic phenomenon, iteration is always optional. Can iteration be predicted from any attribute of the context of situation? It is relatively easy to demonstrate this possibility when some obligatory elements are iterative. For example, there is the possibility of iteration for SR and SC as indicated by Text 4.2. Essentially, the iteration of these can be predicted on two assumptions:

Iteration is always optional.

1. the customer does not remember all the goods at once; and/or
2. the vendor must display readiness to serve and continue to invite more SRs, due to the nature of the field and tenor. This acts as an incentive to further SR.

A guess can be made about the motivation for the iteration of SE. Whatever goods or services are required, the recipient of these—here, the customer—needs to be sure that they are of the type desired. This can involve repeated queries because:

1. phenomena possess more than one attribute; and/or
2. any one attribute may be discussed and elaborated upon.

Text 4.2 has another optional element, FINIS (= F). The probability of its occurrence is higher when the social distance between the participants moves towards the minimal end of the scale. The element has a function that Malinowski would have described as 'phatic communion'. It is not a signal to end the purchase act; this was achieved in PC. F is a signal that although the purchase act—an experiential event—is completed, the interpersonal relation continues. This is done by a display of good will: *have a nice day*, and/or the expression of the desire to renew contact: *see ya*.

Finis is optional.

One optional element that did not appear in Text 4.2 is GREETING (G). G is like F in that it indicates continuity of personal relation, signalling the recognition of the other participant as a potential agent in some activity.

A text and its genre: generic structure potential

In the discussion above I have established:

1. the obligatory elements for Texts 4.1 and 4.2;
2. the optional elements for Text 4.2;
3. the iteration of elements in Text 4.2.

I have also stated the order of sequence for the obligatory elements and implied what the order would be for some of the optional ones, for example, F and G. Some more will be said below about the sequence of other optional elements. Here I would like to compare Texts 4.1 and 4.2, and arrive at some generalisations through this comparison.

We find that Texts 4.1 and 4.2 are closely related: they are embedded in the same CC and share the same set of obligatory elements. These two points of similarity are interdependent. Generally speaking, language is doing the same kind of job in both—it is assisting in the buying and selling of some goods of a specific kind. There are differences too; these can be expressed very briefly as the kind of differences that do not alter the kind of job that language is doing. Structurally, Text 4.2 contains certain elements that could be contained but need not be contained in other texts embedded in the same context. It is possible

optional and obligatory elements and structure potential

to express the total range of optional and obligatory elements and their order in such a way that we exhaust the possibility of text structure for every text that can be appropriate to CC1. In other words it is possible to state the STRUCTURE POTENTIAL of this genre, or its GENERIC STRUCTURE POTENTIAL. The acronyms SP and GSP will be used inter-

GSP = generic structure potential.

changeably to refer to this from now on. The GSP for CC1 is shown in Table 4.4.

Table 4.4 Generic structure potential for CC1

$$[(G)\cdot(SI)\hat{\ }]\ [(\overset{\frown}{SE}\cdot)\ \{SR\hat{\ }\overset{\frown}{SC}\}\ \hat{\ }S\hat{\ }]P\hat{\ }PC(\hat{\ }F)$$

You will recognise the labels for structures and the caret sign indicating sequence. The round brackets indicate optionality of enclosed elements: so G, SI, SE, and F are optional. Any one—or more—of these elements may or my not occur in some text embedded in CC1. The dot · between elements indicates more than one option in sequence.

Optionality never implies complete freedom.

But optionality of sequence is never equal to complete freedom; the restraint is indicated by the square bracket. So, for example, we can read the first square bracket as follows:

- G and/or SI may/may not occur;
- if they both occur, then either G may precede SI, or follow it;
- neither G nor SI can follow the elements to the right of SI.

The curved arrow shows iteration. Thus $(\overset{\frown}{SE}\cdot)$ indicates that:

- SE is optional;
- SE can occur anywhere, so long as it does not precede G or SI and so long as it does not follow P or PC or F;
- SE can be iterative.

So, together with iteration and optionality of sequence, SE is projected as capable of occurring before, after, and/or between the three other elements in the square bracket.

The braces with a curved arrow $\{\overset{\frown}{\ }\}$ indicate that the degree of iteration for elements within the braces is equal; if SR occurs twice, then SC must also occur twice; and so on.

A GSP of the type presented in Table 4.4 is a condensed statement of the conditions under which a text will be seen as one that is appropriate to CC1. It is a powerful device in that it permits a large number of possible structures that can be actualised. Let us refer to

actual structure

any one actualisation of GSP as ACTUAL STRUCTURE. We have already met two actualisations of the GSP: Texts 4.1 and 4.2, both of which display an actual structure the possibility of which is captured in the GSP. These actual structures are represented in Table 4.5:

Table 4.5 The actual structures of Texts 4.1 and 4.2

Text 4.1: SR$\hat{\ }$SC$\hat{\ }$S$\hat{\ }$P$\hat{\ }$PC

Text 4.2: SI$\hat{\ }$SR$_1\hat{\ }$SC$_1\hat{\ }$SE$_1\hat{\ }$SE$_2\hat{\ }$SR$_2\hat{\ }$SE$_3\hat{\ }$SC$_2\hat{\ }$S$\hat{\ }$P$\hat{\ }$PC$\hat{\ }$F

Text 4.3 is another example.

Text 4.3

V:	Good morning, Mrs Reid.	⌐G
C:	Good morning, Bob.	⌐
	Can I have a couple of apples?	⌐SR
V:	Is that all today?	⌐SC
C:	Yes thank you.	⌐
V:	Sixty cents.	⌐S
C:	Here y'are.	⌐P
V:	Thank you.	⌐PC
	Goo'day.	⌐
C:	'Bye.	⌐F

The actual structure of Text 4.3 can be represented as follows:
$$G^\char`\^SR^\char`\^SC^\char`\^S^\char`\^P^\char`\^PC^\char`\^F$$

Another text may begin with an SE, 'How much are those Granny Smiths today?', and might then follow the pattern of Text 4.3 from SR onwards to PC, and so on.

Even restricting ourselves to just the elements SE, SR, SC, and S and ignoring the possibility of iteration, we can get at least the following fragments of texts appropriate to CC‡ (see Texts 4.4-4.7).

Text 4.4

SE: Have you any Granny Smiths? Yes, large or medium?
SR: Well give me half a dozen large ones please.
SC: Yes, what else? That's all, thanks.
    actual structure = . . . SE^SR^SC . . ..

Text 4.5

SR: Can I have half a dozen large Granny Smiths?
SE: Are they local? They look very good. Yes, they are from the Blue Mountains.
SC: Will that be all now? Yes, thank you.
    actual structure = . . . SR^SE^SC . . ..

Text 4.6

SR: Can I have a dozen Granny Smiths?
SC: Will that be all now? Yes.
SE: Where are these apples from? They look very good.
    actual structure = ... SR^SC^SE . . ..

Text 4.7

SR: Can I have a dozen Granny Smiths?
SC: Will that be all just now? Yes, thank you.
S: That'll be 95 cents.
SE: Where are these apples from? They look very good.
    actual structure = . . . SR^SC^S^SE . . .

Each of these texts has a different actual structure, but each realises a possibility built into the GSP.

The significance of this point is discussed in Chapter 6.

The status of obligatory elements in the structure potential

A particular GSP is recognised by the set of obligatory elements; this claim is implied in the observation that optional elements have wider applicability. This makes it important to distinguish between optional and obligatory elements. Let us see if this is possible.

An interesting fact about the obligatory elements appears to be that they are open to certain kinds of operations. These can be seen as strategies for ensuring that:

- the obligatory elements do occur;
- that their realisation is adequate.

Strategy: probe

See p. 59.

Consider CC1. Suppose a customer enters a shop and just hangs about making no SR. What is likely to happen? Very possibly, the vendor would say 'Can I help you?', 'Are you all right?', or some such thing. This is our familiar element SI and it can be seen as a strategy to provoke an SR. While it is not binding on the customer that, in response, he or she—let's say she—make a sale request, this strategy forces her to come clean. Either she must take on the role of a looker-on— 'No, I'm just looking'—or she must produce a sale request or sale enquiry. We could perhaps refer to this strategy as PROBE. It consists of some device that is calculated to bring about the kind of behaviour on the part of some (one) participant that could reasonably be read by the others as a manifestation of an obligatory element in question, or if appropriate, it may lead to a claim that the view of the CC held by the other participant should be revised. 'I am just looking' is equal to saying 'this is not a shopping situation for me'.

Strategy: repair

A second strategy is that of REPAIR. This strategy is employed when an obligatory element is realised, but not adequately. For example if in CC1, a buyer says 'I'd like some oranges', this will be an inadequate realisation of SR. The vendor cannot proceed to the next stage without more information and is likely to repair the situation by saying 'Would a 3 kilo bag be enough?' or 'Did you want navels? They are five for ninety-nine'. So this is a strategy to lead to the adequate realisation of an obligatory element.

Strategy: re-align

In those CCs where the social distance is tending towards minimal, talk can get diverted from one direction to another in face-to-face interaction. So even if the field is 'economic transaction: purchase', the vendor and customer may find themselves engaged in a discussion that bears no specific relevance to the matter in hand. One may move from a discussion of strawberries, to that of drought, to that of high cattle mortality, to that of the government's ineptitude in handling the situation. There are strategies for bringing the wandering participant back to the business in hand by joking, by confronting, and by taking the topic and deliberately relating it to something in hand (Cloran, 1982). More work needs to be done to check whether these strategies—which we may call RE-ALIGN—are normally applied only so that an obligatory element occurs, thus ensuring return to the CC in question.

A characteristic of obligatory elements

If we ask why it is possible to use probe or repair for obligatory elements, the answer will highlight the main difference between these and the optional elements. Knowledge of the CC provides a very good idea of what meanings are relevant to what stage of an ongoing activity, and if those meanings are not being made at that stage, something can be done about it. For example, no utterance can act as SR unless it contains information about the identity and quantity of the commodity sought. So if either of these features is missing from the utterance seeking commodity, repair can be applied. By contrast, we can only do something fairly general and indeterminate about an optional element, for example, SE. This element may concern the availability, and/or the attributes, and/or the cost of the commodity; and even this does not exhaust the possibilities. So when faced with a novel product, a buyer may want to know how it should be used, how much might be sufficient, and so on.

Although I have said a good deal about the obligatory elements, we shall return to the notion, and also to that of the relation between text and context, in Chapter 6. Let us examine very briefly here the question of the realisation of the elements of text structure.

The realisation of structural elements

There is a good reason for establishing some certain way of defining the boundaries of a text's structural elements. Without this, the analysis will remain so intuitive that two persons analysing the same text might differ greatly. So it is desirable to find criteria for deciding what part of a text realises which element; more than that, it is important to establish what type of criteria these are.

One thing that seems quite certain is that no neat one-to-one correspondence exists between a structural element and a clause or sentence. In Text 4.2, the element SI is realised by clauses (1) and (2). Nor See p. 61. does one structural element correspond to one speaker turn; it is not the case that one turn by one speaker will necessarily contain just one element of text structure. SI in Text 4.2 covers one full turn (*Who's next?*) and one half (*I think I am*), after which the rest of the customer's turn is devoted to the realisation of the next element, SR. Nor is the structural element always co-extensive with one individual message or act. Greeting and Finis always require two individual acts—for example, a greeting and a greeting back. The search for a unit of some sort—either syntactic (for example, sentence), dialogic management (for example, turn), or message status (for example, offer—receipt)—as a

Elements of structure
are defined in a
specific CC.

universal formal equivalent of a structural element seems doomed to failure. The text is a unit of meaning; it is language that is functional in some context. If this is true, then the elements of the structure of the text will have to be defined by the job they do in that specific contextual configuration, which is logically related to the text's structure. And this implies (1) that the realisational criteria need not be identical across genres, and (2) that an element's realisational criteria might be stated most clearly in terms of some semantic property. For example, we can say that SR must be realised by the following set of semantic properties:

- demand
- reference to goods
- quantity of goods.

See p.54.

Even with an optional element, it is possible to make certain claims that may be sufficient for its identification; for example, SE must make reference to the same general domain in which the participants are operating. In Text 4.1, we could not have an SE such as 'What size shoes do you wear?' or 'Do you like to go sailing?'. I am not suggesting that these sorts of unrelated things cannot be said. But if they are, it is highly likely that the participants as well as the onlookers will regard them not as a part of the buying—selling text, but rather as a separate one.

Context, genre, and text structure

To think of text structure not in terms of the structure of each individual text as a separate entity, but as a general statement about a genre as a whole, is to imply that there exists a close relation between text and context, precisely of the type that has been discussed in the preceding pages. The value of this approach lies ultimately in the recognition of the functional nature of language. If text and context are related in the ways I have argued above, then it follows that there cannot be just one right way of either speaking or writing. What is appropriate in one environment may not be quite so appropriate in another.

Further, there is the implication that an ability to write an excellent essay on the causes of the Second World War does not establish that one can produce a passable report on a case in a court of law. This is not because one piece of writing is inherently more difficult or demanding than the other, but because one may have more experience of that particular genre.

The early stages of essay writing are probably quite as problematic—and for exactly the same reason—for all youngsters (Martin & Rothery, 1980, 1981; Christie, 1983). One learns to make texts by making texts, in much the same way as one learns to speak a language by speaking that language. Familiarity with different genres does not grow automatically with growing age, just as language does not simply happen because you are two or three or five years old. For both you need social experience.

Learning to construct
texts is a matter of
social experience.

A child may not experience at home the genres that the system of education particularly requires. In this respect, home environments

68

might differ significantly. The home where a child naturally encounters different kinds of written communication creates an awareness of language that is not the same as that created by a 'print-less' home. But the school requires the same types of tasks to be performed by all its pupils. A teacher's understanding of generic structures will be an active ingredient in his or her success as a teacher. Children need to be exposed to a wide range of genres—particularly those that are actively required in the educational process—for example, résumé, report, expository essay, and so on. It is a mistaken view of both text and learning to imagine that one can get children to write an essay on the relationship between climate and vegetation by simply talking about it; and it is worse still to imagine that one can do this without talking about it at all.

This is not a contradictory statement. In the earlier part of this chapter, I suggested that the spoken mode is more versatile than the written. This is not an accident. Many—in fact most—of our activities are conducted through speaking (Goffman, 1974, 1981). Talk prepares the way into the written mode. But it would be a mistake to think that writing something down is simply a matter of putting down graphically what you could have said phonically. The structures of written and spoken genres vary a great deal even if they might range around the same, or a similar, field. It is one thing to talk about text structure to a group of students and another to write about it for the same kind of audience. The case of the child in the classroom is no different. The child needs to be given the experience of both talking and writing over a large range of genres.

The relevance of structure to recall and comprehension is another important fact. A passage of writing has a better chance of being remembered if its structure is clear. In language studies—particularly where early reading and writing are concerned—often the pupil is exposed not to clear, well-structured texts, but to a jumble of nonsensical sentences, for example, 'Dan can fan', 'Man can fan', 'Dan can fan man' (Gerot, 1982). Such items still appear in many early readers.

An understanding of text structure and the relevance of text structure to understanding and recall will be sufficient to deter any teacher from the use of such material, which instead of helping the child actively puts a hurdle in his or her way!

Chapter 5

The texture of a text

Introduction

I began the last chapter with the claim that unity is a crucial attribute of texts, and went on to examine one source of textual unity: namely, structure. I tried to show that the structure of a text is closely related to the context of situation, so much so that the specific values of field, tenor, and mode, which together make up a contextual configuration, can be used to make certain predictions about the structure of the text, just as the unfolding structure of the text itself can be used as a pointer to the very nature of the contextual configuration. There is, thus, a two-way relationship between text structure and contextual configuration: the on-going structure of the text defines and confirms the nature of the contextual configuration, while the latter acts as a point of reference for deciding what kind of elements can appropriately appear when, where, and how often.

In this chapter we shall look at the second source of textual unity: namely, texture.

What is texture?

Texture, like structure, can be shown to be ultimately related to the context of situation. This is a theme that I shall come back to in Chapter 6. Here, let me begin by a brief discussion of two examples (Examples 5.1 and 5.2).

Example 5.1
Once upon a time there was a little girl
and she went out for a walk
and she saw a lovely little teddybear
and so she took it home
and when she got home she washed it.

Example 5.2

He got up on the buffalo
I have booked a seat
I have put it away in the cupboard
I have not eaten it.

Faced with these two examples, any natural speaker of English is bound to say that Example 5.1 displays certain continuities that are lacking in Example 5.2. One of these continuities is, of course, describable in terms of generic structure. Although the first passage is incomplete, it is a clear instance of a familiar genre; we have no difficulty in recognising it as an unfinished story. It is, however, doubtful if Example 5.2 will be seen as representative of a genre quite so readily, though many of us who have taught a foreign language might not be surprised to find that the four sentences of Example 5.2 have been lifted from a foreign language teaching exercise. Now, even if we were to accept that a foreign language teaching exercise represents a genre, it appears undeniable that such a genre would not possess structure in quite the same sense as that discussed in the preceding chapter. For one thing, there is no discernible beginning, middle, and end in such exercises. In fact, due to deplorable misconceptions about language, the continuities in a language teaching exercise are normally strictly meta-textual; there is a purely formal reason for grouping the sentences of Example 5.2 together, which has very little to do with language as used in everyday life.

But structural continuity is not the only kind of continuity; Examples 5.1 and 5.2 differ in another important respect; I would talk of this difference in terms of texture. Thus I would claim that the first of these examples possesses the attribute of texture, and that this attribute is lacking in the second. What kind of continuities do I have in mind when making such a claim? To answer this question, let us examine these examples a little more closely. Note that the first has certain kinds of meaning relations between its parts that are not to be found in the second. It is these meaning relations that are constitutive of texture. For example, the third person, feminine, singular pronoun *she* in each of its occurrences refers to the same little girl to whom the nominal group *a little girl* refers; *it*, on the other hand, refers to the same lovely little teddybear to which *a lovely little teddybear* refers. A more concise way of saying the same thing is that *she* is co-referential with *a little girl*, and *it* is co-referential with *a lovely little teddybear*. If we compare the two occurrences of *it* in Example 5.2 with those in 5.1, we note an important difference: it would make no sense to claim that *it* in either of its occurrences in 5.2 is co-referential with any other item in the example. This is definitely not the whole story, but perhaps enough has been said to draw certain conclusions:

Texture is a matter of meaning relations.

1. The texture of a text is manifested by certain kinds of semantic relations between its individual messages. The nature of these relations and the lexico-grammatical patterns that realise them are discussed in the following sections.

2. At least in the first instance, texture and text structure must be seen as separate phenomena. We know that from the point of view of text structure, Example 5.1 is incomplete, but this does not affect the claim that it has texture. So to say that a passage possesses texture is not to make any claim about the specific structural status of that passage. The relationship appears to operate only in one direction: whatever is (part of) a text must possess texture; it may or may not be a complete (element of a) text.

3. The property of texture is related to the listener's perception of coherence. Thus in common parlance, Example 5.1 would be described as possessing coherence while Example 5.2 would be seen as lacking in coherence. A discussion of the notion of coherence is presented below.

Texture, cohesive ties, and cohesive devices

The exaggerated difference between Examples 5.1 and 5.2 might lead one to suppose that coherence is an all-or-none phenomenon. This is decidedly not true, as a reading of Texts 5.1 and 5.2 will demonstrate.

Text 5.1
1. once upon a time there was a little girl
2. and she went out for a walk
3. and she saw a lovely little teddybear
4. and so she took it home
5. and when she got home she washed it
6. and when she took it to bed with her she cuddled it
7. and she fell straight to sleep
8. and when she got up and combed it with a little wirebrush the teddybear opened his eyes
9. and started to speak to her
10. and she had the teddybear for many many weeks and years
11. and so when the teddybear got dirty she used to wash it
12. and every time she brushed it it used to say some new words from a different country
13. and that's how she used to know how to speak English, Scottish, and all the rest.

Text 5.2
1. the sailor goes on the ship
2. and he's coming home with a dog
3. and the dog wants the boy and the girl
4. and they don't know the bear's in the chair
5. and the bear's coming to go to sleep in it
6. and they find the bear in the chair
7. they wake him up
8. and chuck him out the room
9. and take it to the zoo
10. the sailor takes his hat off
11. and the dog's chased the bear out the room
12. and the boy will sit down in their chair what the bear was sleeping in.

It would be untrue to claim that Text 5.2 is entirely incoherent or that is possesses no texture, though it is equally obvious that the text is less coherent than is Text 5.1. This raises two questions:

1. How do Texts 5.1 and 5.2 differ in their texture, if they do?
2. If the two vary in the degree of coherence, what, if any, patterns of language correlate with this variation?

In the sections below, I attempt to answer these questions. However, before we can examine and compare the specific texture of Texts 5.1 and 5.2, we need to be clear about the semantic and lexico-grammatical patterns essential to the creation of texture in general. I shall discuss the linguistics of texture before I return to the two questions I have raised.

Cohesive tie

In talking about texture, the concept that is most important is that of a TIE. The term itself implies a relation: you cannot have a tie without two members, and the members cannot appear in a tie unless there is a relation between them. Let us draw a picture of the tie:

If you think of a text as a continuous space in which individual messages follow each other, then the items that function as the two ends of the tie—the A and the B—are spatially separated from each other; A may be part of one message and B part of another. But there is a link between the two, depicted above by the two-headed arrow. The nature of this link is semantic: the two terms of any tie are tied together through some meaning relation. Such semantic relations form the basis for cohesion between the messages of a text. There are certain kinds of meaning relation that may obtain between the two members. For instance, take the first two lines of the rhyme in Example 5.3.

Semantic relations are the basis of cohesion.

Example 5.3

I had a little nut tree
Nothing would it bear
But a silver nutmeg
And a golden pear.

Then thinking of *little nut tree* in line 1 as member A and *it* in line 2 as member B you can see that the semantic relation between the two is the identity of reference. The pronoun *it* refers to no other nut tree but the one that has already been mentioned as *a little nut tree*; the situational referents of both are the same thing. In the literature on the discussion of textual continuity, this relationship of situational identity of reference is known as CO-REFERENTIALITY.

co-referentiality

Imagine now that we have two other sentences (see Example 5.4).

Example 5.4

I play the cello. My husband does, too.

Then following the earlier practice, we could say that *play the cello* is member A and *does* is a member B of the cohesive tie. But this time the relationship is not of referential identity. The cello playing that I do is a different situational event from the cello playing that my husband does. So the relation here is not of co-referentiality, but of the kind that could be described as CO-CLASSIFICATION. In this type of meaning relation, the things, processes, or circumstances to which A and B refer belong to an identical class, but each end of the cohesive tie refers to a distinct member of this class. Thus there is a significant difference between co-referentiality and co-classification.

co-classification

A third kind of semantic relation between the two members of a tie is exemplified by *silver* and *golden* in the last two lines of Example 5.3. Here the relationship is neither of co-reference nor of co-classification; it is, rather, that both refer to something within the same general field of meaning. Thus both silver and gold refer to metal, and within metal to precious metal—their primary class affiliation is not identical—unlike two separate acts of playing the cello—but there is a general resemblance. For want of a better term, I refer to this kind of general meaning relation as CO-EXTENSION.

co-extension

These three semantic relations of co-referentiality, co-classification, and co-extension are precisely what ties the two members of a tie, and the existence of such ties is essential to texture. The longer the text, the truer this statement.

Cohesive devices—co-reference and co-classification

These semantic relations are not independent of the lexico-grammatical patterns. It is not the case that they can be established randomly between any two types of language units; instead, there are very strong tendencies for a specific relation to be realised by a clearly definable set of items. For example, the relation of co-referentiality is typically realised by the devices of reference, such as the pronominals 'he', 'she', 'it', etc. or by the use of the definite article 'the' or that of the demonstratives 'this' or 'that'. By contrast, co-classification is normally realised either by substitution or by ellipsis. I should emphasise, perhaps, that this is a statement of what is typical; it does not describe all cases. Either of the devices can realise either of the relations, but it is more typical for reference type devices to signify co-referentiality and for substitution and ellipsis to signify the relation of co-classification. I have already given an example of substitution in Example 5.4; an example of ellipsis is given in the mini-dialogue Example 5.5.

Example 5.5

ellipsis

—'Can I borrow your pen?'
—'Yes, but what happened to yours?'

Here the nominal group *yours* is elliptical and its non-elliptical version would be 'your pen'. Note that my pen and your pen are two distinct objects; they belong to the same class, but they are two distinct members of the class. Thus the realisation of these two semantic relations—i.e. co-referentiality and co-classification—typically involves two distinct types of lexico-grammatical patterns.

There is, however, something in common to the lexico-grammatical patterns that typically realised these two semantic relations: and this something that is in common can be pointed out by looking more closely into the nature of the member B of each tie type (see Figure 5.1).

Figure 5.1

	A	B		tie type
Example 5.3	little nut tree	it	=	co-referential
Example 5.4	plays the cello	does	=	co-classification
Example 5.5	your pen	yours	=	co-classification

Member B of each of these ties is an item to which we can refer as an implicit encoding device. What this means is that the specific interpretation of *it*, *does*, and *yours* is not possible in the same way as that of *nut tree*, *husband*, *cello*, and *pen* is. The interpretation of this latter set is possible without referring to any other item of the text; this is patently not true with such items as *it*, *the*, *my*, *this*, *do so*, and *yours*. Their interpretation has to be found by reference to some other source. And it is this essentially relational nature of the implicit encoding devices that endows them with the possibility of functioning as a COHESIVE DEVICE.

cohesive device

Such devices become cohesive—have a cohesive function and so are constitutive of texture—precisely if and when they can be interpreted through their relation to some other (explicit) encoding device in the same passage. If the source for their interpretation is located within the text, then a cohesive tie of the type(s) discussed above is established; the establishment of such a tie creates cohesion. In our earlier work (Halliday & Hasan, 1976) such cohesive devices have been referred to as GRAMMATICAL COHESIVE DEVICES.

Recall that we have a third type of cohesive tie—the type in which the semantic relation is that of co-extension. Before embarking on a discussion of the nature of the linguistic units that can act as terms in this third kind of tie, I would like to take up a question here that arises from the recognition of implicit encoding devices.

Implicit devices and their interpretation

In the above discussion, I pointed out that an implicit encoding device is essentially relational; its interpretation has to be found by reference to some other source. This raises the question of where the interpretative source is to be found, and an examination of that question will force us to revise some of the comments made earlier about the terms of the tie; at the same time it will add another parameter to our understanding of tie types.

Our earlier chapters have sought to demonstrate the functional nature of language, and the close relationship that exists between context and text structure. It follows, then, that any linguistic unit from a text that we focus on has two environments: (1) the extra-linguistic environment—the context—relevant to the total text; and (2) the linguistic environment—the co-text—the language acompanying the linguistic unit under focus. So, the source for the interpretation of the implicit encoding devices could either be co-textual or purely contextual.

endophoric ties

The interpretation is said to be ENDOPHORIC (Halliday & Hasan, 1976) when the interpretative source of the implicit term lies within the co-text as, for example, with *she* and *little girl* or *it* and *nut tree*. It is really the endophoric ties that are crucial to the texture of a text: unless an endophoric interpretation of the implicit term can be sustained, cohesion would not be perceived. Note that in Example 5.2, it is impossible to sustain an endophoric interpretation of any of the implicit devices.

Given the fact that language unfolds in time, the linguistic units of a text occur in succession. This permits a further factoring of endophoric interpretation. Whatever implicit term is under focus may either follow or precede that linguistic unit by reference to which it is interpreted—i.e. its LINGUISTIC REFERENT. When it follows its linguistic referent, the label given to such a cohesive tie is ANAPHORIC (Halliday & Hasan, 1976). Every example of cohesive tie (except that between *silver* and *golden*) provided so far in this chapter has been anaphoric. When the implicit term precedes its linguistic referent, the cohesive tie thus established is known as CATAPHORIC (Halliday & Hasan, 1976). An illustration is given in Example 5.6.

anaphoric reference

cataphoric reference

Example 5.6

I shall be telling this with a sigh
Somewhere ages and ages hence:
Two roads diverged in a wood, and I—
I took the one less travelled by,
and that has made all the difference.

This is the last stanza from Robert Frost's 'The road not taken'. Here the demonstrative *this* of the first line will be interpreted by reference to lines 3-5 of the stanza. So there exists a cataphoric co-referential cohesive tie between *this* and lines 3-5.

exophoric reference

The interpretation of an implicit device is said to be EXOPHORIC when the source for its interpretation lies outside the co-text and can only be found through an examination of the context. Imagine a situation in which a small child is hammering away at some toy, making a good deal of noise while the mother is trying to concentrate on writing a conference paper. It is highly probable that she might say to the child:

Example 5.7

Stop doing that here. I'm trying to work.

The first message of Example 5.7 is highly implicit; and none of the items *doing*, *that*, and *here* can be interpreted except by reference to the immediate context of situation. Exophorically interpreted implicit devices create an opaque link between the text and its context so

76

far as speakers outside the context are concerned. The degree of opacity is obviously variable (Hasan, 1984c), but if all the implicit devices in a passage could only be interpreted exophorically, then to an outsider, the passage would appear either to lack all texture, or if it is perceived as possessing texture, it would be because of cohesive ties with the semantic relation of co-extension.

See pp. 79–82.

Cohesive interpretation and cohesive tie

One last point needs to be made before turning to co-extension, and this is as follows: the interpretation of the implicit term must be seen as an issue that is, in principle, separate from the kind of semantic relation between the terms of the tie. It is possible to determine the kind of semantic links between the two terms of a tie, even though the intended specific meaning of the terms might not be available. Consider Examples 5.8 and 5.9.

Example 5.8

They asked the sailor for some food
and he gave them a loaf of bread.

Example 5.9

I don't want this one
I want that one.

Most of us when faced with Example 5.8 will treat *them* in the second message as co-referential with *they* even though we would have no idea whether the two refer to 'two children' or 'some beggars' or whatever. Thus we would say that there is a cohesive co-referential tie between *they* and *them*, which is not a claim that could be made about *they* and *them* in Example 5.10.

Example 5.10

They asked the sailor for some food
and he found *them* in the bottom of the bag.

The reason why most speakers would not think of *them* as co-referential with *they* in Example 5.10 is furnished by their understanding of English language. Turning to Example 5.9, we would treat *one* in the second message as co-classificational with *one* in the first. This treatment would not be possible if Example 5.9 were to be rewritten as Example 5.11.

Example 5.11

I don't want this one
so you can have it.

I have laboured this point because
1. it throws a new light on some of the statements made in the previous sections 'Cohesive devices' and 'Implicit devices and their interpretation';

2. it raises the question of the basis of perceiving the semantic relations of co-reference and co-classification; and
3. it is relevant to the role of exophoric devices in creating texture.

To take the first point first, I said earlier that cohesion is established when an implicit device is interpreted by reference to some item of the text. This is true so far as it goes, but Examples 5.8 and 5.9 clearly demonstrate that a cohesive link can be established even when the specific meaning remains unknown. This demonstrates that what is more important to texture is the identity and/or the similarity of the semantic content rather than the content itself. The interpretation of a term *it* by reference to another term *nut tree* creates texture not because the interpretation has become available, but because the interpretation clinches the fact that a particular kind of semantic relation obtains.

So how about exophora? Are exophorically interpreted items an embarrassment to this approach to texture? Whenever scholars have attempted to prove that it is possible to have texts without cohesion, in order to demonstrate their point they have normally created what I would describe as 'minimal texts' consisting of either a single message by one participant, or one message per participant. Now, since the status of text as text is functionally defined, in principle, it is irrelevant what number of messages a text contains. However, in describing the attributes of a class of phenomena we need to start with typical members; and it cannot be denied that discourse whether spoken or written is typically productive of much larger—non-minimal—texts, which display the full range of possibilities open to texts in general. By contrast, taking the minimal text as typical, we would be forced to concede many points that it would be absurd to have to concede. For example, we might have to say that texts do not have generic structure; and to concede this is quite absurd. So in order to support our statements about texts in general, we must take non-minimal texts into account, since this will permit generalisations about minimal texts as well, while the reverse is not true.

A case in point are those implicit devices—'he', 'she', 'it', etc.— which have no specific linguistic referent within the text. When the text is minimal as in Example 5.7, it appears impossible to arrive at the interpretation of such devices except by reference to the context of situation. Moreover, the devices seem to enter into no cohesive relation with any other linguistic items in the text. However, if we examine longer texts, we find that both these conditions are an artefact of the size of the text. Implicit encoding devices **can** be intepreted without recourse to situational clues even in the absence of a specific linguistic referent in the text. In fact, sometimes, this is the only possibility open to us in poetic texts. Consider an extract from Tomlinson's lyric, whose title is just 'Poem' (see Example 5.12).

Example 5.12

Upended, it crouches on broken limbs
About to run forward. No longer threatened
But surprised into this vigilance
It gapes enmity from its hollowed core.

Moist woodflesh, softened to a paste
Of marl and white splinter, dangles
Where overhead the torn root
Casts up its wounds in a ragged orchis.

Throughout this poem, the word 'tree' never appears, yet a practised reader is bound to interpret *it* (line 1) and *its* (line 4) as tree. Since, in the case of literary texts, appeal to the immediate situation is patently impossible, it follows that the interpretation has been arrived at due to some feature(s) of 'Poem'. And here the importance of such expressions as *hollowed core, woodflesh, splinter, and torn root* cannot be denied. Note also that the reader will perceive the semantic relation of co-referentiality between *it* (line 1), *it*, and *its* (line 4). One might claim that these items are, after all, not exophoric, since their referent is determined text-internally; however, there is no specific linguistic referent of *it* present in the entire text. Even conceding that the pronominals are exophoric does not force us to accept that they are irrelevant to texture. In the following poem, 'A slumber did my spirit seal', by Wordsworth, *she* is definitely exophoric, but the relations between the three instances of *she* are still cohesive (see Example 5.13).

Example 5.13

A slumber did my spirit seal;
I had no human fears:
She seemed a thing that could not feel
The touch of earthly years.

No motion has she now, no force;
She neither hears nor sees;
Rolled round in earth's diurnal course,
With rocks, and stones, and trees.

As in the case of Tomlinson's stanza, so here it can hardly be denied that the perception of continuity presupposes the perception of a relation of co-reference between the pronominals. I want to put forward the hypothesis that the interpretation of items in the absence of a linguistic referent and/or any situational clues as well as the perception of semantic relation between un-interpreted implicit devices is made possible because of the third type of tie—that which is based on co-extension. Where such ties do not exist, the relation of co-reference and co-classification are at least problematic if not impossible to establish. This brings us to the discussion of the nature of the linguistic units that can act as the terms of a co-extensional tie.

Cohesive devices — co-extension

Let us go back to Example 5.3.

Figure 5.2

	A	B		tie-type
Example 5.3	silver	golden	=	co-extension

Compare the tie in Figure 5.2 with the three ties laid out in Figure 5.1. See p. 75.
You will immediately note an important difference: neither of the terms

in this tie is implicit; we do not need to refer to anything else in order to interpret the terms *silver* and *golden*—we only need to know the language. The two terms of a co-extensional tie are typically linguistic units that we refer to as 'content words' or 'lexical items'. The relation of co-extension, described earlier, naturally does not exist between any two randomly co-occurring lexical items. So we need to state under what conditions such a relation comes about. 'The same general field of meaning' is a vague expression. And if we leave the expression unelaborated, then any kind of meaning association could be taken as constituting a relation. We could end up with a chain in which the members of the tie were as follows: flower, petal, stem, stalk, twig, branch, trunk, tree, wood, log, faggot, tinder, fire, flame. In this list we have ended up grouping items such as 'flower' and 'flame', between which it is not very easy to say what kind of general meaning relation obtains. But if we examine the list, we would find that in this collection there is no point at which we could stop on the ground that the members of the pair are not related meaning-wise. The members of each consecutive pair such as, say, 'flower' and 'petal', 'petal' and 'stem', and 'stem' and 'stalk' show a close meaning relation, but the further apart the items are the more difficult it is to relate them to each other semantically; for instance, consider 'flower' and 'faggot'. So obviously what we have to do is to delimit the notion 'general field of meaning'.

To achieve this end, I have used the traditional concept of sense relation with certain additions. The three sense relations generally recognised in the literature on semantics are those of SYNONYMY, ANTONYMY, and HYPONYMY. Whenever two lexical expressions stand in any of these relations, a cohesive tie is established.

In SYNONYMY, the experiential meaning of the two lexical items is identical; this does not mean that there is a total overlap of meanings, simply that so far as one kind of meaning goes, they 'mean the same'. The standard literature in semantics, for example, mentions such pairs as 'woman' and 'lady', 'buy' and 'purchase', and 'smile' and 'grin', etc.

ANTONYMY can be described as the oppositeness of experiential meaning; the members of our co-extensional tie *silver* and *golden* are an example of this kind of meaning relation.

HYPONYMY is a relation that holds between a general class and its sub-classes. The item referring to the general class is called SUPER-ORDINATE; those referring to its sub-classes are known as its HYPONYM. If we take *animal* as an example of super-ordinate then its hyponyms are *cat*, *dog*, *bear*, etc. Note that *cat*, *dog*, and *bear* are also semantically related as the co-hyponyms of the superordinate *animal*.

The lexicon of a language is organised into a hyponymic hierarchy, so that we have differing degrees of generality. For example, in English, the most general and therefore the super-ordinate *par excellence* is the item 'thing', which can be used to refer to almost anything. Consider also the gradation of generality in *food, fruit, berry, blueberry*. At this point let me draw attention to the fact that when we have a relation of co-hyponymy, as for example, between *cat* and *dog*, we can also think of the relation as that of weak antonymy. The distinction between a certain kind of antonymy and co-hyponymy is not easy

three sense relations

synonymy

antonymy

hyponymy

to draw. On the other hand, this matters little for our immediate purposes, since whether the two items are related as antonyms or as co-hyponyms, the relation will contribute to cohesion in either case.

To these generally recognised sense relations, I would add that of MERONYMY: the term refers to a part—whole relation as in the case of *tree*, *limb*, and *root*, where *limb* and *root* are co-meronyms, naming parts of the superordinate *tree*. While meronymy is very much like a sense relation, there is another kind of lexical patterning that contributes to texture but, strictly speaking, is not recognised as a kind of sense relation. I have in mind the REPETITION of the same lexical unit. The repetition of the same lexical unit creates a relation simply because a largely similar experiential meaning is encoded in each repeated occurrence of the lexical unit as in Example 5.14.

[margin: meronymy]

[margin: repetition of lexical items]

Example 5.14

There were children everywhere.
There were children on the swings, children on the slides, and children on the merry-go-round.

It is also possible to have repetition where the morphologically distinct forms of the same lexical unit occur. In Example 5.15 the items *suggested* and *suggestion* are really two distinct morphological forms of the same lexical unit and can be treated as a case of repetition.

Example 5.15

The committee suggested that all sexist language be removed from the regulations. If this suggestion is adopted, we shall have to avoid 'he', 'his', etc.

This discussion of the cohesive devices has been necessarily brief and does not cover all the devices recognised in Halliday & Hasan (1976) or in Hasan (1979; 1984b). So I shall add two comments:

1. All lexical cohesive devices discussed above are general in nature. For example, the relation of synonymy between *lady* and *woman* is a general fact of English. There are cohesive devices that are entirely specific to a single text, for example, those of INSTANTIAL SEMBLANCE as in *all my pleasures are like yesterdays* (Hasan, 1984b).

   The continuities created by structural devices have not been mentioned, for example PARALLELISM (Halliday & Hasan, 1976), and the organisation of Theme-Rheme and Given-New (Fries, 1983).

2. All devices discussed are COMPONENTIAL. The items that serve as terms of a tie form part of some message(s), i.e. they are message components. The linking of components creates cohesion between messages. But there is a large number of devices known as cohesive conjunctives (Halliday & Hasan, 1976; Martin, 1983) that contribute to texture. These devices are ORGANIC; the terms in the tie are whole message(s) rather than message components, for example, in the following, where one whole message is consequence and the other cause: *I'm going to bed 'cause I'm very sleepy.* Adjacency pairs, for example question—answer, request—compliance (Schegloff, 1968; Goffman, 1975), are a variety of organic cohesive device.

81

Table 5.1 summarises the devices discussed.

Table 5.1 Summary of cohesive devices

NON-STRUCTURAL COHESION

COMPONENTIAL RELATIONS		ORGANIC RELATIONS
Device	Typical tie relation	A: **Conjunctives**

<table>
<tr><td rowspan="6">GRAMMATICAL COHESIVE DEVICES</td><td>A: Reference
1. Pronominals
2. Demonstratives
3. Definite article
4. Comparatives</td><td>co-reference</td><td>A: Conjunctives
e.g. causal tie
concession tie ...</td></tr>
<tr><td>B: Substitution
& Ellipsis
1. Nominal
2. Verbal
3. Clausal</td><td>co-classification</td><td>B: Adjacency pairs
e.g. Question (followed by) answer;
offer (followed by) acceptance;
order (followed by) compliance ...</td></tr>
<tr><td rowspan="2">LEXICAL COHESIVE DEVICES</td><td>A: General
1. Repetition
2. Synonymy
3. Antonymy
4. Meronymy</td><td>co-classification
or
co-extension</td><td>Continuatives
(e.g. still, already...)</td></tr>
<tr><td>B: Instantial
1. Equivalence
2. Naming
3. Semblance</td><td>co-reference
or
co-classification</td><td></td></tr>
</table>

STRUCTURAL COHESION

A: **Parallelism**
B: **Theme-Rheme Development**
C: **Given-New Organisation**

The interdependence of grammatical and lexical cohesion

I suggested before that even if two implicit terms remain un-interpreted, as in Examples 5.8 and 5.9, it is still possible to perceive relations of co-reference and co-classification between them. With Example 5.12 I drew attention to the fact that even in the absence of both a specific linguistic referent and any situational clues, there are occasions when it is possible to provide an interpretation of the implicit device. I went on to suggest that both these things happen largely because of the semantic relations maintained through lexical ties. In a text of non-minimal size, there normally occur many such threads of semantic relation, and their simultaneous operation is important in the resolution of both the above problems. The moral from this is easy to draw: to be effective, grammatical cohesion requires the support of lexical cohesion.

However, the relationship is not so one-sided: to be effective, lexical cohesion, in its turn, requires the support of grammatical cohesion. The reciprocity of these two kinds of cohesion is essential, as can be seen from Examples 5.16 and 5.17.

Example 5.16

John gets up early. We bought him a tie. He loves peaches. My house is next to his.

Example 5.17

A cat is sitting on a fence. A fence is often made of wood. Carpenters work with wood. Wood planks can be bought from a lumber store.

In Example 5.16 there is no grammatical reason that would prevent *he*, *him*, and *his* from referring back to *John*. But if I say that *him* in the second sentence of this example should be interpreted as *John*, you just have to take it on faith; there is nothing in the text that points you in the direction of that particular interpretation. Why? Because grammatical cohesion is not supported here by lexical cohesion; the relations discussed under 'Co-extension' do not tie any two lexical items of Example 5.16. By itself, grammatical cohesion does not work. On the other hand, lexical cohesion does not work by itself either. In Example 5.17, we find only lexical cohesive relations: of reiteration, synonymy, and hyponymy. Thus we have *fence* and *wood* reiterated, and we have *lumber* and *wood planks*. None the less, it is an odd kind of text, if text it is. In comparison with Example 5.16, we may perhaps be willing to think of it as more of a text, but by no stretch of the imagination could we think of it as a typical one.

In a typical text, grammatical and lexical cohesion move hand in hand, the one supporting the other. The many differing kinds of semantic relations operate at one and the same time through sizeable portions of a text. To demonstrate this point, let me examine in some detail the first five clauses of Text 5.1. In Figure 5.3 each rectangle stands See p. 70. for one clause. Within each of these clauses there are components that enter into a grammatical or lexical cohesive relation. There are four such threads of continuity:

1. the first, with the first element *girl* in clause 1;
2. the second, with *went* in clause 2;
3. the third, with *teddy bear* in clause 3; and
4. the fourth, with *home* in clause 4.

Figure 5.3

cl. 1 cl. 2   cl. 3   cl. 4   cl. 5

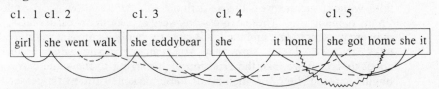

Each of these form part of a CHAIN in which the members are related to each other in specific ways. To indicate the movement of the chain, I will connect the members of the first chain with a solid line; those of the second with dots; those of the third with dots and dashes, while the links in the fourth chain will be indicated with a wavy line. Each rectangle contains only those components of the clause that function as elements or links in the chain. Figure 5.3 demonstrates the appropriateness of the metaphor 'threads of continuity running throughout the text' to describe the simultaneous operation of many cohesive chains, each of which supports and refines the domain of meaning for the others. This is one reason why, in natural uses of language, we hardly ever notice ambiguities.

cohesive chains

A technical term that has appeared in this discussion is COHESIVE CHAIN. What is a cohesive chain? As the analysis provided in Figure 5.3 shows, a chain is formed by a set of items each of which is related to the others by the semantic relation of co-reference, co-classification, and/or co-extension. Taking the type of relation into account, we can sub-categorise chains into two types: IDENTITY CHAINS and SIMILARITY CHAINS. Again, both of these are exemplified in Figure 5.3. Thus chain 1 with *girl*, *she*, etc. is an identity chain. The relation between the members of an identity chain is that of co-reference: every member of the chain refers to the same thing, event, or whatever, as in this chain, where each item refers to the same girl. This particular identity chain is text-exhaustive, i.e. it runs from the beginning to the end of the text. This, I would suggest tentatively, is a characteristic of short narratives: texts of this category normally contain at least one text-exhaustive identity chain.

an identity chain

a similarity chain

Now, turning to similarity chains, an example of which is provided by chain 2 in Figure 5.3 with *went*, *walk*, etc.: the members of a similarity chain are related to each other either by co-classification or co-extension. Each such chain is made up of items that refer to non-identical members of the same class of things, events, etc., or to members of non-identical but related classes of things, events, etc.

The distinction between identity and similarity chains is important, relating both to the notion of text and of context. Let us take the identity chain first. Each item in an identity chain refers to the same 'thing' (where the word 'thing' should be interpreted as covering any class of referent). Paradoxically, however, the extra-linguistic identity of the thing is immaterial to texture. Let me develop this point a little. While writing this chapter I have used such items as *I*, *me*, *my*. These make an identity chain, each item in the chain referring to the same extra-linguistic thing: Ruqaiya Hasan. Now, independent of this text, Ruqaiya Hasan is the same person who will be talking to students at Macquarie University in a few week's time. I find that it is not possible to give talks without such expressions as 'I find . . .', 'let me show . . .', and 'in my opinion . . .'. These expressions were present in my earlier talks, they are present today, and they will most probably be present in future talks as well. I am sure that you can anticipate what I am about to say: if we take the criterion of 'referring to the same extra-linguistic thing' literally, then all of these variants of the first person singular pronoun will form but one identity chain. Such an identity chain may definitely have uses in the construction of biographies and case histories, but it is quite useless so far as notions of textual unity and textual identity are concerned. So we come up with the rather interesting conclusion that the notion 'the same extra-linguistic thing' must be modified by the expression 'within the context of this specific text', rather than being taken as a text-independent entity.

The members of a similarity chain are related by co-classification and/or co-extension. In Figure 5.3, a similarity chain occurs with members *went*, *walk*, and *got* (i.e. reached); the relationship between these items is not identity of reference but similarity of reference, so that the referents lie within the same general field of meaning. For example, walking is a kind of going, and going is an important part of getting anywhere.

There is one rather significant difference between similarity and identity chains. If two texts embedded in the same contextual configuration are compared, we are highly likely to find a considerable degree of overlap in at least some of the similarity chains found in them. This is not an accident. The items in a similarity chain belong to the same general field of meaning, referring to (related/similar) actions, events, and objects and their attributes. The lexical items in a general field of meaning form a semantic grouping that represents the potential for the formation of similarity chains. This semantic grouping is genre-specific and to the extent that similarity chains are really a part of the total semantic grouping, they too are genre-specific. The implication is that if we know the specific social process—the field of discourse—relevant to an interaction, it will be possible to predict that some selection from this or that semantic grouping will appear in the shape of similarity chains in the text generated; equally, selections from given semantic groupings are constitutive of the field of discourse. So semantic groupings are logically related to specific contextual configurations, though how much of such a grouping will appear in the shape of similarity chains in a particular text of a given genre is open to variation.

difference between similarity and identity chains

By contrast, identity chains, particularly when their terms refer to some specific individual—person(s) or object(s)—rather than to a whole class as such, are essentially accidental from the point of view of the contextual configuration. So far as appointment making is concerned, it matters little whether the patient is Smith or Wilson, whether the receptionist is Glen or Anderson. This does not imply that identity chains are unimportant; in fact, in certain genres, they appear to be rather closely related to the overall structural shape of a text (Hasan, 1984b).

The above sections were concerned with the presentation of some of the major cohesive devices that contribute to texture. In the following section, I address the first question raised earlier regarding Texts 5.1 and 5.2: how do they differ, if they do, in respect of their texture? To answer this question, I shall restrict myself to such notions as have been presented above in some detail. I shall ignore instantial lexical cohesion, all organic relations, and all forms of structural cohesion (see Table 5.3). This is not because they are less important, but because time and space are limited.

This question is raised in the section entitled 'Texture, cohesive ties, and cohesive devices', p. 73.

The texture of Texts 5.1 and 5.2

See pp. 70, 71.

Look again at Texts 5.1 and 5.2.

Whenever I have presented these two texts to informants, they have unanimously agreed that Text 5.2 is less coherent than 5.1 (which is not to say that 5.2 is a non-text). An explanation of what this judgment correlates with in patterns of texture is difficult to find, so long as grammatical and lexical cohesion are examined separately. You will probably be surprised to learn that the number of grammatical cohesive devices in the two texts is identical as shown in Tables 5.2 and 5.3.

Table 5.2 Grammatical cohesive devices in Text 5.1

2.	she	3.	she
4.	she it	5.	she she it
6.	she it her she it	7.	she
8.	she SE it the his	9.	SE her
10.	she the	11.	the she it
12.	she it it	13.	she ⁺the***

Table 5.3 Grammatical cohesive devices in Text 5.2

1.	⁺the ⁺the	2.	⁺he
3.	the ⁺the ⁺the	4.	they? ⁺the ⁺the
5.	the it	6.	they? the the
7.	they? him	8.	SE? him ⁺the
9.	SE? it ⁺the	10.	the his
11.	the the the	12.	the their? the

As is obvious from Tables 5.2 and 5.3, the texts do not differ crucially in the frequency of grammatical cohesive devices; nor do they differ greatly in the patterns of lexical selection, or even in the proportion of devices that are subsumed in chains. Table 5.4 presents some facts regarding grammatical and lexical cohesion in the two texts.

Table 5.4 Grammatical and lexical cohesive devices in Texts 5.1 and 5.2

		Text 5.1	Text 5.2
1.	grammatical cohesive devices	30	30
2.	frequency of 1 per clause	2.3	2.5
3.	percentage of 1 entering in chains	97	93
4.	explicit lexical tokens	47	37
5.	cohesively interpreted lexical tokens	27	30
6.	total lexical tokens	74	67
7.	5 as percentage of 6	36	41
8.	percentage of 1 interpreted anaphorically	97	60
9.	percentage of 1 interpreted exophorically	3	27
10.	percentage of 1 phorically ambiguous	—	13

SE = subject ellipsis.

Let me first gloss the unfamiliar terms. SE in Tables 5.2 and 5.3 stands for subject ellipsis; the first example occurs in message 8 of Text 5.1:

when she got up
and [SE] combed it

where SE will be interpreted as *she*, i.e. (aforementioned) *little girl*. In message 13 of Text 5.1, *the* has several asterisks (*) attached to it; this is to sensitise you to the fact that it occurs in a semi-fixed expression *all the rest*. In Table 5.3, several grammatical devices have an interrogative (?) or a cross (+) attached to them; the former is to indicate that the interpretation of these is problematic—they could be interpreted in more than one way; the cross is to indicate that the device is exophoric. Table 5.4 (line 3) presents percentages of grammatical cohesive devices entering in chains; these chains are formal as described in Halliday & Hasan (1976) and do not necessarily correspond to identity and/or similarity chains. The term 'explicit lexical token' refers to the content words in the texts, which appear as content words from the start; by contrast 'cohesively interpreted lexical tokens' are those that are arrived at when the grammatical cohesive devices (of Tables 5.2 and 5.3) are interpreted.

Tables 5.5 and 5.6 present the total picture. In these two tables, those lexical items are underlined that are the interpretation of some grammatical cohesive device. For example, in Table 5.5, message 2, *girl* is underlined; this lexical item is the interpretation of *she* from message 2 of Text 5.1: *she went out for a walk*. You will note that some items are underlined with broken lines; each of these is a noun modified by *the*. For example, Text 5.2, line 1, reads: *the sailor goes on the ship*. Given the meaning of *the* (Halliday & Hasan, 1976; Hasan, 1984c), the modified noun refers to a uniquely identified (set of) thing(s). The cross (+) marks exophorically interpreted *the*.

Table 5.5   Lexical rendering—Text 5.1
1.   little girl was
2.   girl went walk
3.   girl saw lovely little teddybear
4.   girl took teddybear home
5.   girl got home girl washed teddybear
6.   girl took-to-bed teddybear girl girl cuddled teddybear
7.   girl fell-to-sleep straight
8.   girl got-up girl combed teddybear little wirebrush teddybear opened-eyes teddybear
9.   teddybear started speak girl
10. girl had teddybear many many years weeks
11. teddybear got dirty girl washed teddybear
12. girl brushed teddybear teddybear say some new words different country
13. girl know speak English Scottish all-+the-rest***

Table 5.6   Lexical rendering — Text 5.2
1.   +sailor go +ship
2.   sailor come home dog
3.   dog want +boy + girl
4.   sailor boy girl dog know +bear was +chair
5.   bear come go-to-sleep chair
6.   sailor dog boy girl find bear chair
7.   sailor dog boy girl wake-up bear
8.   sailor dog boy girl chuck-out bear +room
9.   sailor dog boy girl take bear +zoo
10. sailor take-off sailor hat
11. dog chased bear room
12. boy sit sailor dog boy girl chair bear sleep

Returning now to Table 5.4, line 7 shows what percentage of the total lexical tokens is arrived at through the interpretation of the grammatical cohesive devices. So far the differences between Text 5.1 and 5.2 have been statistically insignificant, but the last three entries appear different. Of the grammatical cohesive devices of Text 5.1, 97 per cent are anaphorically interpretable. This means that the text is highly self-sufficient; to understand the speaker's meanings, one needs simply to know the English language. Not so, with Text 5.2, where 40 per cent of the devices cannot be interpreted by reference to the text; 27 per cent are exophorically interpretable while 13 per cent are ambiguous.

Text 5.1 is highly self-sufficient.

question 2, p.73

'If the two vary in the degree of coherence, what, if any, patterns of language correlate with this variation?'

We are now in a position to revive question 2 raised at the beginning of this chapter, rephrasing it, in the light of our findings, as follows: can the listener's perception of varying degrees of coherence between Texts 5.1 and 5.2 be correlated with the differences in texture indicated in the last three entries of Table 5.4?

Texture and textual coherence

Exophora

See 'Cohesive interpretation and cohesive tie', p. 77.

There can be no unequivocal answer to the question raised above. I have argued above that although exophora reduces the possibility of interpretation, it does not necessarily prevent the formation of cohesive ties; and to this extent it does not militate against texture, particularly if we find that relations of co-reference and/or co-classification are not being adversely affected by the presence of exophora. What is the position with regard to Text 5.2?

the origins of Texts 5.1 and 5.2

Here the history of the data is relevant. These stories were collected in Bernstein's Sociological Research Unit (University of London) in the mid-1960s from children who were asked to tell a bedtime story to a teddybear about a sailor, a dog, a boy, and a girl. All five characters were presented in toy form to the children. Thus the meaning of *the* in *the sailor* type of phrase was clear to both participants. Moreover, in all cases the exophoric device is *the*. In a group such as *the sailor*, someone who does not know the history of the data is likely to ask: which sailor? However, it is doubtful that the absence of an answer to this question will make the reader perceive Text 5.2 as less coherent, especially since the co-referential link between *the sailor* of line 1 and *the sailor* of line 10 does not appear to be in question. There are altogether eight occurrences of exophoric *the* (see Table 5.3 and 5.6, items with cross mark (+)) where a new referent is introduced exophorically, for example *the sailor, the ship* (line 1), *the boy, the girl* (line 3). Of these only *the ship* (line 1), *the room* (line 8), and *the zoo* (line 9) did not appear in the instruction given to the child. The exophora of *the zoo* is a formal exophora (Hasan, 1984c) which is the least opaque of the exophorics; *the ship* and *the room* become less problematic because of the semantic relation between *sailor* and *ship* and *home* and *room*. If Text 5.2 is perceived as less coherent than Text 5.1, the reason cannot lie in the variation of exophorically interpreted grammatical devices.

Ambiguity

What is the position with regard to ambiguity? Ambiguity appears to be more relevant. An ambiguous grammatical cohesive device is one that could be interpreted in more than one way given the frame of the particular text. In Text 5.2, there are six such devices; they occur in lines 4, 6, 7, 8, 9, and 12 (see Tables 5.3 and 5.6). The source of their ambiguity is the same, so we need discuss only *they* from line 4. In lines 1-3 of Text 5.2, we are introduced to *the sailor*, *a dog*, *the boy*, and *the girl*. One possible reading of *they* is that it is co-referential only with *the boy and the girl*; another is that it is co-referential with all four on the ground that *dog* is quasi human; and a third possibility is that *they* is co-referential only with the humans. I would disregard the last possibility because its motivation is a non-textual notion of what the world is like. But even so, it is not easy to decide between the first and second alternative. On the principle that the probability of pronominals being co-referential with the nearest appropriate nominal group— simplex or complex—is the highest, it would be reasonable to interpret *they* as *the boy and the girl*.

Nothing in the text disturbs this interpretation, until we come to think about the fate of the sailor and the dog. On this interpretation of *they*, sailor and dog have no role in the story until we get to lines 10 and 11. Line 11 shows that dog could very well be included amongst those who chuck the bear out of the room; chasing out and chucking out are, after all, part of the same general activity. In line 10, the sailor may be said to be, metaphorically, mopping his brow; you could say he takes his hat off after the completion of a rather demanding exercise. This interpretation has the merit of saving the sailor from just hanging around doing nothing between lines 1 and 10 of the text. On these grounds, it seems far more reasonable to interpret *they* of line 4 as co-referential with *sailor*, *dog*, *boy*, and *girl*.

Neither of the interpretations is without its problems; if we adopt the last one, as I have done, this is only because I wish to give maximal benefit of the doubt to the child-author of this story. But in doing this, one must not forget the problems that remain unresolved. An interesting question is: under what conditions does ambiguity of the type under discussion arise? It is quite possible that such ambiguity and relative lack of coherence are the product of the same factors, and that there is no direct logical relationship between ambiguity and relative lack of coherence. If this is the case, then it should be possible to find texts that are lacking in coherence without also displaying ambiguities. In my work with children's stories, I have found that lack of coherence can exist independently of ambiguity, and that if the text is coherent, a certain degree of ambiguity can be tolerated (Hasan 1984b).

Cohesive chains

I argued that lexical cohesive relations are instrumental in permitting the interpretation of those implicit items that lack both a specific linguistic referent, and a situational clue. This implies that lexical cohesive relations are relevant to any discussion of the sources of the kind

See 'Cohesive interpretation and cohesive tie', p. 77.

See p. 82.

See 'The inter-
dependence of
grammatical and lexical
cohesion', p. 82.

of ambiguity under focus. The discussion regarding 'The interdependence of grammatical and lexical cohesion' also carries the same implication. It might therefore be illuminating to look into the identity and
similarity chains formed in the two texts. Perhaps this examination
would at once provide an explanation for the occurrence of ambiguity
and reduced coherence. Table 5.7 presents the chains from Text 5.1.

Table 5.7 Cohesive chains in Text 5.1

Identity chains:	(a)	girl (17)
	(b)	teddybear (14)
	(c)	home (2)
Similarity chains:	(d)	was got (= became)
	(e)	went walk got (= reached)
	(f)	lovely dirty
	(g)	wash (2) comb brush
	(h)	took had (= owned)
	(i)	weeks years
	(j)	many (2) some
	(k)	new different
	(l)	speak (2) say
	(m)	took-to-bed fell-to-sleep got-up opened-eyes
	(n)	words English Scottish all-the-rest
	(o)	little (3)

The numbers in brackets show how many tokens of the lexical unit
occurred in the text. Of the total tokens, 90.5 per cent (67 out of 74)
are subsumed in cohesive chains. How does this compare with Text 5.2?

Here we face a problem. It is difficult to decide what goes into the
identity chains and what the total set of lexical tokens for Text 5.2 is,
without resolving the ambiguity. One solution is to ignore those identity chains relating to *sailor*, *boy*, *girl*, or *dog*, and examine the rest
of the text. In that case, our findings will be as displayed in Table 5.8.

Table 5.8 Cohesive chains in Text 5.2

Identity chains:	(a)	bear (8)
	(b)	chair (4)
Similarity chains:	(c)	come (2) go take
	(d)	go-to-sleep wake-up sleep
	(e)	find chase-out chuck-out
	(f)	home room (2)

When *sailor*, *dog*, *boy*, and *girl* are ignored, the total number of
lexical tokens in Text 5.2 is reduced to 33; of these 25 are subsumed
into chains. By comparison with Text 5.1, only 76 per cent of the tokens
are in cohesive chains. In respect of cohesive chains then there seems
to be a significant difference between Texts 5.1 and 5.2. But what is
the interpretation of this difference?

One obvious interpretation is that lexical selections in Text 5.2 do
not divide themselves into a homogeneous set of semantic groupings.
The fairly large percentage of tokens that fall outside chains—i.e. are
PERIPHERAL—prevent a consistent reconstitution of the field of the text.
This can then be seen as part of the reason why Text 5.2 coheres less
well than Text 5.1.

90

Chain interaction

Convincing as this explanation seems, it just will not work; though, no doubt, there is a good deal of truth in it. In the first place the high percentage of peripheral tokens does not necessarily entail ambiguity; Example 5.17 has only 64 per cent of its lexical tokens in chains, yet it contains no ambiguity. True, it could not be described as a coherent text. But the fact that a high percentage of lexical tokens are RELEVANT—i.e. enter into chains—does not necessarily entail coherence. There is no better proof of this than a list such as follows.

Example 5.18

girls bananas two spend shopkeeper
apples own girls dollars grapes
buy fifty sell cents shopkeeper
girls fruit

No one could possibly describe this list as a coherent text, though 100 per cent of its tokens are subsumed in chains. So we are still far from any linguistic fact that can be unequivocally correlated with variation in coherence.

It is important to recall here that in constructing chains, we are concerned with components of messages. Our entire analysis has revolved around components rather than whole messages as such. On the other hand, it is only message as message that has any textual viability; and it is only at the rank of clause or above that a lexico-grammatical unit is contextually viable: it is only at this rank—or above—that a linguistic unit can encode a complete message. Although the chains go a long way towards building the foundation for coherence, they are not sufficient; we need to include some relations that are characteristic of those between the components of a message. This is the relation that I refer to as CHAIN INTERACTION.

chain interaction

By chain interaction I mean relations that bring together members of two (or more) distinct chains. These relations are essentially grammatical. For example, if we take chain (a) *girl* and chain (e) *went*, *walk*, *got* from Table 5.7, we would note that *girl* is in an identical grammatical relation with *went* and *got*—*girl* is the ACTOR of the ACTION *went* and *got*. We can say, then, that in Text 5.1, chains (a) and (e) interact. A minimum requirement for chain interaction is that **at least two members** of one chain should stand in the same relation to **two members** of another chain. This requirement is important for two reasons:

1. The relations that lead to chain interaction are the very ones that exist between the constituents of a clause or of a group, for example, doer, doing; sayer, saying; doing, done-to; or quality, qualified, etc. If a single such relation were considered sufficient for chain interaction, then by definition every member of the chains would interact with some member. This would be tantamount to saying that anything that is a clause or a group is, *per se*, responsible for coherence. Moreover, there would be no need to differentiate between chain formation and chain interaction; since the former by itself

91

would be a measure of chain interaction. But this is surely wrong since a random list of clauses or groups would not necessarily be coherent; nor does chaining entail coherence (see discussion of Example 5.18 above).

2. The second reason is deeper still. The recurrence of a relation between two chains is indicative of two vectors of unity. The first vector of unity is indicated by the semantic similarity that permits members to be part of the same chain; the second vector of unity indicates the semantic similarity that unites at least pairs of members from two chains. The rationale for this is simple to find: in a coherent text one says similar kinds of things about similar phenomena. For example, the girl in Text 5.1 does not simply go home, she also gets home; she does not simply fall asleep, she also wakes up, and so on.

When the text is not too long, the chain interaction within it can be visually displayed. This visual display highlights the continuities and the discontinuities in the text. Figures 5.4 and 5.5 display the chain interaction in Texts 5.1 and 5.2 respectively.

Figure 5.4   Chain interaction in Text 5.1

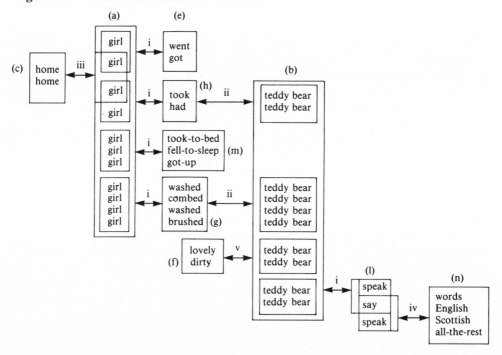

Each rectangle in these figures represents a (part of a) chain; the chain labels used here are the same as in Tables 5.7 and 5.8. If Figure 5.4 is compared with Table 5.7, you will see that (a) *girl* contains 17 members, though the rectangle (a) in Figure 5.4 contains only 11 of these: this is because only 11 of the 17 members of chain (a) qualify as interacting with some other chain(s). Thus although the rectangles bear chain labels, they need not represent complete chains. When there

Figure 5.5 Chain interaction in Text 5.2

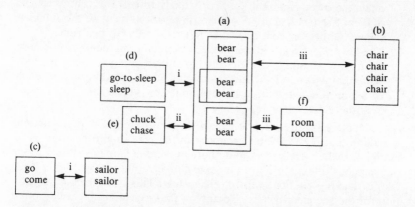

is chain interaction, two items of each chain interact with two items of at least one other; each interacting segment of the chain—two or more members—is boxed together to make the interaction display easier to follow. Thus in Figure 5.4, the first and second entries of *girl* interact with (e) *went* and *got*; the second and third *girl* entries interact with (c) *home*; the third and fourth *girl* entries interact with (h) *took*, *had*, and so on.

Each arrow in these figures has a roman number to allow easy reference. They can be glossed as follows:

Any two chains linked by an arrow marked

i   are in 'actor action' relation (for example, *girl went*);
ii   are in 'action acted-upon' relation (for example, *took teddybear*)
iii are in 'action and/or actor location' relation (for example, *girl got home*)
iv   are in 'saying text' relation (for example, *said words*)
v   are in 'attribute attribuand' relation (for example, *lovely teddybear*)

Those members of the chain that enter into interaction (and would thus appear in displays of the type shown in Figures 5.4 and 5.5) are known as CENTRAL TOKENS; the remaining members of the chain are NON-CENTRAL. We thus have the following classification of the total lexical tokens of a text:

1. Relevant tokens: All tokens that enter into identity or similarity chains; relevant tokens
    these divide into: central tokens
    (a) Central tokens: those relevant tokens that interact;
    (b) Non-central tokens: those relevant tokens that do not interact; non-central tokens
2. Peripheral tokens: All those tokens that do not enter into any kind peripheral tokens
    of chain, for instance *cuddled* in Text 5.1 and *hat* in Text 5.2.

Having established the framework throughout this section, we can now linguistic correlates of
state fairly definitely what the linguistic correlates of variation in variation in coherence
coherence will be:

1. The lower the proportion of the peripheral tokens to the relevant ones, the more coherent the text is likely to be. Note that in Text 5.1, relevant tokens form 90.5 per cent of the total while in Text 5.2, they make up only 76 per cent.

93

2. The higher the proportion of the central tokens to the non-central ones, the more coherent the text is likely to be. The central tokens of Text 5.1 (see Figure 5.4) constitute 65 per cent of the relevant tokens while for Text 5.2, this figure is only 36 per cent.
3. The fewer the breaks in the picture of interaction, the more coherent the text. In Figure 5.4, the entire set of interacting chains is related, with chains (a) and (b) functioning as FOCAL CHAINS, chains each of which interacts with a large number of other chains. In Figure 5.5, there is a clear break.

focal chains

The three features mentioned above are ordered. The first amounts to saying that the semantic grouping in the text should be such as to establish unequivocally certain definite referential domains. If and when this happens, the majority of the lexical tokens of a text will fall within chains, leaving out but an insignificant few. This is a necessary condition for the second attribute. Texture is thus essential to textual unity, and cohesion is the foundation on which the edifice of coherence is built. Like all foundations, it is necessary but not sufficient by itself.

The second statement amounts to the claim that simply the establishment of the definite referential domains is not enough. Identity and similarity should not be limited to message components alone—such identity and similarity underlie chain formation; the notions of identity and similarity should also be extended to the content of the message as message. In common parlance, when speakers are engaged in the process of creating a coherent text, they stay with the same and similar things long enough to show how similar the states of affairs are in which these same and similar things are implicated.

The third statement claims that the process of creating coherent texts involves an indication of relationships between the things one is 'on about'. The outcome is that a complete break in chain interaction does not take place—transition from one topic to the next is a merging rather than a clear boundary.

cohesive harmony

I have referred to the sum of these three phenomena as COHESIVE HARMONY; and a briefer claim about coherence could be formulated thus:

variation in coherence is the function of variation in the cohesive harmony of a text.

It is harmony in more than one respect: it brings together lexical and grammatical cohesive devices, subjecting them to semantic considerations of identity and similarity. This is as it should be; a text, after all, is not a unit of form but of meaning. Secondly, it is harmony because it harmonises the output of two macrofunctions: the textual and the experiential. The output of the textual function are the chains and the interactions; the output of the experiential function at the rank of clause and group is what the interaction is built upon. Thus cohesive harmony is an account of how the two functions find their expression in one significant whole. No doubt, the concept of cohesive harmony can be further refined by bringing in the logical and interpersonal functions into the picture. If this can be done, it will show that even where text is concerned, multifunctionality is a fruitful concept.

Texture, coherence, and the teacher

In recent years, some objections have been raised to this approach. For example, it is said (Morgan, 1978; de Beaugrande, 1980) that coherence is ultimately based on the assumption that when speakers speak they say things that cohere with each other. True, we do make such an assumption. But this does not absolve us from asking: what is this assumption itself based upon? What are the conditions under which such an assumption cannot be sustained by a listener? Why do we have to abandon such an assumption in the case of some speakers, for example, that of Text 5.2? Questions of this kind can be answered if the issues of texture and coherence are approached in the manner I have suggested; instead of taking the basis for granted, our approach probes the very basis of the basis. And in all practical applications, this is a significant difference.

One very important aspect of education is the production of coherent discourse. A teacher aims to educate and train in such a way that the students are able to 'talk about' their selected topics in a coherent and connected way. It is the experience of teachers at all levels—universities not excepted—that the early discourse of students in a new field is relatively less coherent than their later discourse. This is because the semantic relations between the key concepts are not yet clear. A teacher can definitely not start with the assumption of coherence or non-coherence when picking up an exercise by a student. He or she—let's say she—has to take the discourse as it comes, solely on its own merit. And in order to explain to herself why the discourse does not work as the student no doubt wished it to work, the teacher has to look at the meaning relations—including gaps in meaning relations. She can only do this by concentrating on the language of that exercise, as meanings are constructed by language.

some educational implications

What I have said about written exercises, applies *mutatis mutandis* in the case of spoken discourse in the classroom. Gestures, eye contact, and posture are indeed important means of negotiating meanings, but in the domain of education—particularly in explaining, say, the causes of the Second World War, or the relation between ideology and history, or the hidden assumptions of the cult of individuality—the meanings relevant to the matter of the topic must be created through the appropriate, communally interpretable use of language. And that implies by creating a coherent discourse. That, in its turn, implies by understanding meaning relations between the concepts of the chosen field. And that in its turn demands that those who broach these specialist concepts—teachers and authors alike—must in their turn produce coherent discourse. The world, and particularly the world of education, is made up of talk. The success of talk is not something we can just assume. We need to know what properties talk must have in order to be successful. It is one part of this problem that is examined in this chapter.

It would be a gross misunderstanding and misuse of the main message of this chapter to act as if a person can be taught to produce a coherent text by such simplistic methods as, for example, exhorting them to put in 60 per cent of pronominals, 20 per cent of definite articles, 3 causal relations, and by making the lexis hang together in chains. The cohesive devices create texture because they establish relations of meaning. The incoherence of discourse is often a pointer to an inability to organise the relevant meanings in relation to each other. A teacher can assist by pointing out what semantic consequence the choice of a particular pattern of wording has; for example, what difference of meaning there is between the following: *select a tube and put it in the bottle* and *select a tube and put one in the bottle*. It is these kinds of deep semantic differences that the mere assumption of coherence will not and does not handle. The infra-structure of all assumptions about co-operative acts of doing and saying is, in the last resort, social. The **assumption** of coherence can be sustained so well because human language has the resource for indicating coherence, while the nature of language as a resource has developed in a particular way because it has had to serve the needs of the community. Our task is to understand the specific nature of these resources—not simply to hide behind the mind and the intention of particular speakers and listeners.

Chapter 6
The identity of the text

Introduction

The last two chapters were concerned with the kinds of unity that characterise texts. In Chapter 4, I attempted to show how structural unity is relatable to the notion of context. I argued in particular that the motivation for the elements of the text's structure can be found in the values of the CC. This position raises some questions; and most of this chapter will be concerned with exploring these questions.

In Chapter 5, I examined the unity of texture, without specifically relating it to the question of structure or CC. So part of this chapter will be concerned with examining whether such relations exist and, if so, what might be said about them. It may be useful to begin here by stating the problems explicitly.

The identity of a CC

If one claims, as I have done, that the values of a CC motivate the occurrence of an element of text structure—just as the appearance of a certain element gives rise to the inference of a certain value in the CC—then the notion of contextual configuration becomes pivotal to the entire discussion. And the following question assumes importance: how is the identity of a contextual configuration determined? At what point, and with what rationale, do we say 'This is a CC that is distinct from that one'? For example, if in CC1 in the values of field we found 'personal clothing' instead of 'perishable food', would we say that we have a different CC, or is it still to be regarded as another case of CC1? Whatever our answer, how do we justify it? This question is discussed later in this chapter.

See 'The contextual configuration of Text 4.1', p. 59.

The identity of a genre

In Chapter 4, the claim was made that Texts 4.1, 4.2, and 4.3 all belonged to the same genre and that the fragments Texts 4.4—4.7 would also appear within texts of the same genre. This naturally raises the question: how far does the identity of a genre extend? What criteria would we use for establishing generic identity?

See p. 65.

Some other questions that are closely related to this basic one should also be considered. For example, if presented with a text in displacement—in isolation from the situation in which it was produced—we are still able to say what type of text it is. Is it a sermon? Is it a lecture? Is it a buying and selling transaction? Is it to control a child? Is it a story? We are able to classify the instances of texts along these kinds of categories when we come in contact with them. What is there in a text that gives away the secret of its context, its setting? And why is it there?

Not only are we able to classify this way, but we get rather sophisticated. So if we read a letter in a magazine that goes something like this:

Text 6.1

Dear Jinny,

I'm so glad you introduced me to Glo-Quick's Super-Facial. It's just unbelievable what a difference it has made to me in less than a week. I must say it's a new and a very pleasant sensation to be noticed with envious admiration . . .

Reading this, we do not say this is a letter to 'dear Jinny'; we know that in reality it is an advertisement for a cosmetic product. What fetaures are there that lead us to this conclusion? In this text, what is 'of the letter' and what 'of the advertisement'? On what basis do we

dissociation of generic form and generic function

make this dissociation between the generic form and the generic function?

The uniqueness of a text

There is no limit to the number of texts that can be produced. Is each one unique? How do we define uniqueness? Obviously uniqueness cannot be simply physical. Every student who holds a copy of this book holds a unique physical thing, but surely we would agree all have the same text. But are matters always so clear-cut? If someone holds the first unrevised edition of this book, do they have the same text? What

Many texts may be created within one genre.

constitutes uniqueness of a text? However we define uniqueness, we shall come to the conclusion that an infinity of variant texts can be created within any one given genre. The question that arises from this conclusion is an important one indeed: what features of a text must be held constant to hold its genre classification constant? And what features of the text can be varied to allow the construction of variant texts, without varying the genre?

The completeness of a text is simply a side issue of this major problem. If we have the following transcript (Text 6.2), what stages do we infer, for which there is no direct linguistic evidence; and why?

Text 6.2

V: Who's next?
C: I am. Can I have a chicken sandwich?
V: Eighty cents.
C: 'bye.

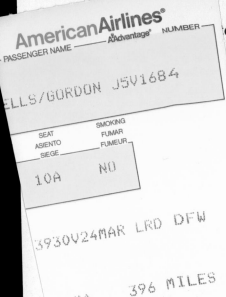

...exture

various cohesive devices, including their
...ty in a text. I referred to this as texture.
...nd structure are related; and if so, how?
...texture might appear somewhat remote
...t structure is the link between the two.
...question is very closely tied to that of
...ments discussed briefly in Chapter 4. See 'The status of obligatory elements in the structure potential', p. 66.
...ns in the order in which they have been

...C?

...iminary but relevant point is the need
...are the notion of 'material situational
...of situation'. The material situational
...nt in which a text might be being
...writing, or reading might be taking
...setting is by no means identical with
...situation relevant to the text. The degree of overlap
between the two is variable, and depends largely on the role of language.
In writing, the overlap between the two is often at its lowest; while in
speech, particularly where the role of language is ancillary, the overlap
is at its highest. Often when people claim that a written text is not dependent on its situation, as for example in the genres of literature, they mean
to refer simply to the fact that their material situational setting does not
impinge upon these texts. In the following discussion, I ignore material
situational setting except where it is co-extensive with context of situation; and I use the term situation as a short form for context of situation. It was necessary to make these distinctions in order to pave the
way to the discussion of the identity of a CC. I intend to do this by
relating it to the concept of CONTEXT OF CULTURE. context of culture

Culture, situation, and CC

As Halliday pointed out in Chapter 1, Malinowski (1923) coined the See pp. 6, 7.
term 'context of culture', as well as 'context of situation'. This was to
highlight the fact that specific contextual configurations themselves
derive their significance ultimately from their relation to the culture to
which they belong. The relationship is not a direct one and can be
presented diagrammatically as in Figure 6.1. In this figure, culture is
shown as the highest abstraction; the left and the right columns are
related to it as a realisation is to the category it realises. The slanting
arrows indicate this relation. So culture is itself more specifically describable as an integrated body of the total set of meanings available to a
community: its semiotic potential. Any meaning system is part of this
resource. The semiotic potential includes ways of doing, ways of being,
and ways of saying. One might say that these are the three general modes three general modes of meaning
of meaning: you can mean by doing, by being, or by saying; and that

99

Figure 6.1   Culture, meaning and situation

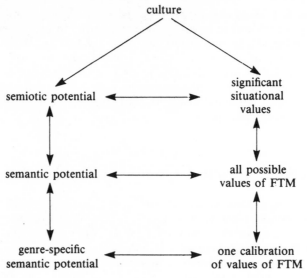

culture

semiotic potential ⟷ significant situational values

semantic potential ⟷ all possible values of FTM

genre-specific semantic potential ⟷ one calibration of values of FTM

Note: F = field; T = tenor; M = mode

over and above this totality of semiotic systems, there is nothing that could be labelled 'culture'; that the semiotic potential **is** culture.

But situations for being, saying, and doing do not exist *per se*; it is not as if there is something inherent in the physical properties of a state of affairs in the external, non-social world that we can recognise as one particular kind of situation. On the contrary, the relationship between the meanings that the various modes construct—the semiotic potential—and the significant situational values is a mutually defining one: situation is not acultural. To give some examples: in the subculture of the Moslems on the Indo-Pakistani subcontinent, there is a situation that is coded in my language by the word 'soyum'. It refers to the third day after the death of a person. Now, logically there is no-one anywhere, after whose death a third day does not physically arrive; but in none of the Western cultures that I am familiar with can this third day be regarded as a 'situation'. For the subcontinental Moslems, however, it is very much a situation: there are ways of being, ways of doing, and things that you say if the 'soyum' concerns you because the deceased was a relative or a friend or even just a neighbour. And these are specific to this situation: it is a situation because it has these meanings associated with it; these meanings are made legitimate by this situation.

Sometimes we are misled simply because of the way we have referred to something; we tend to behave as if the possibility of using the same word implies complete identity between the referents. For example, we go shopping in Myer's, Macy's, or Marks & Spencer's; and we go shopping in the market in Mombasa or Madras. Simply because we have used the words 'go shopping' for both types of event, we might be misled into believing the two events are the same type of thing; that, in fact, they contain the same set of values. Nothing could be further from the truth, as anyone who has had an experience of the markedly different cultures will immediately recognise. The Myer's salesman would be at least surprised, if not affronted, if, at his telling you the price of an object, you responded with *Well, ok, that's fine; but now tell me the real price.* This is precisely the kind of response you are expected to offer at the first telling of the price in a market shop in most parts of the Indo-Pakistani subcontinent. As well as the invitation of the type *Yes, anything else?*, one may encounter direct offers of the type *Do take these guavas as well, they are fresh in today from Malir.* You may even find yourself faced with a bargain: *If you take two kilos of grapes as well, you can have the lot for ten rupees.* The form of address can range from *Saheb/Begum Saheb* (Sir/Madam) to *Bhai Sabeh/Baji* (elder brother/elder sister); and the translation of the native terms into an English phrase with the adjective *elder* should not be seen as indicating age; it simply points to a clear relationship of hierarchy in which the customer is always the top dog, unless he or she forfeits this status by some untoward act or unbecoming appearance.

We can and do use the words 'go shopping' for the service encounter in shops both in a Western capitalist country, for example, Australia, and in a mainly non-industrialised Third World country, for example, Pakistan. But it is important to remember that the ways of saying, being, and doing are qualitatively different in the two politico-economic cultures. Neither the range of appropriate meanings nor the set of significant situational values is the same. This is what it means to say that a given context of situation—a CC—has meaning only within a culture. There is no such situation in the absolute as 'going shopping'.

The first layer of Figure 6.1 claims that a culture is expressed by the totality of what is meaningful; this domain of meaning has been formed by the various semiotic systems—systems that cover ways of being, saying, and doing. These formed meanings construct significant situational values; and it is the operation of the semiotic systems that permits the perception of what is or is not a significant situational variable. Equally, once the significant situational variables have been stabilised—for example, society has got into the way of recognising age, status, wealth, and learning as vectors for hierarchic division—the perception of the values of these different variables will provide the frame for the appropriate exchange of meanings. The horizontal arrow between the two entries of the same layer indicates this bi-directional relationship. What is on the left has come into being to serve the needs set up by the perception of what is on the right; equally, what is on the right has come into being, has acquired a status, because of what is on the left.

Semiotic potential and contextual potential

We could have left the diagram at this point, because it has already said all that is essential. The reason for introducing the next two layers is our specific interest in the relationship between CC and just one semiotic system, namely language. The vertical arrows linking the layers within each column are indicative of a 'subset' relation. So semantic potential is a subset of semiotic potential: it refers only to those meanings that are formed by, and which can be expressed through, language. So at this layer, we have separated out saying from being and doing. Equally, in the right column, we are concerned only with all the values of field, tenor, and mode. The claim is that in the construction of these values, language has played an important role. Halliday draws attention to the very close relation between the situational variables and the lexico-grammatical system. The system of language is so designed that the variables—field, tenor, and mode—will be inevitably encapsulated into the text through the simultaneous encoding of the experiential, interpersonal, and textual meanings.

See Figure 2.4, p. 26.
See Figure 3.4, p. 36.

Generic semantic potential and unique CC

See Chapter 4, p. 56.

We meet the concept CC at the last layer of the diagram. In Chapter 4, I described CC as 'a specific set of values that realises field, tenor, and mode'. It is one particular calibration of the values—one of those systematically permitted by the possibilities open to the three variables. At this point, then, we are back with our initial question: wherein lies the uniqueness of a CC? The answer suggested by the previous discussion is obviously that a particular CC is known by the set of meanings associated with it. It is this set of meanings that we refer to as 'genre-specific semantic potential'.

Now, theoretically, this is a perfectly satisfactory answer, but in practice, it poses some problems because the term 'meaning' is not determinate enough. What kind of meanings are we talking about? There is a difference between the meanings 'banana' and 'bread'. Would the meaning 'bread' be outside of the genre-specific semantic potential associated with CC1? And is this the kind of semantic difference that makes a difference to the identity of the CC? If it is, then we must also accept that, even if all other values of CC1 were held constant, we would still be faced with different CCs according to whether we are buying bananas rather than apples; or two apples rather than one; we should end up with five CCs, none of which would be identical with the others. But such a view of the uniqueness of situation is rather hard to justify. Moreover, on this view, logically we should seldom encounter the same CC twice.

See p. 64.

The best means of getting out of this impasse is to think of a CC not as the statement of **one specific situation**, but rather as the expression of **a type of situation**. So CC1, instead of referring to any one single social activity, is a type that can be instantiated by many instances. What we are looking for are the significant similarities between these many instances. At the same time, it is important to attach greater weight to the word 'potential' in the expression 'genre-specific semantic potential'. By definition, this formulation commits us to the notion of variation. Something can be a potential only if there is the possibility of a choice between this or that. If x always entailed y, we would not be accurate in claiming that x has the potential y. The semantic potential is a potential precisely because it can be stated as a resource—as a range within which variant selections are possible. If this were not the case we would have to say that there is some semantic restriction imposed by some contextual values, rather than that there is some set of possible meanings that can be viewed as a resource for construing some contextual value.

Keeping this very important fact in mind, when we examine the genre-specific semantic potential, we would find at least two general kinds of meaning: those that are relevant as components of the individual messages within the genre, and those that are relevant to the structuring of the overall message form of the texts within the genre. The former kind of meanings are the ones that at the degree of great specificity appear coded as, say, 'two apples' as opposed to 'one apple'; or 'bananas' as opposed to 'apples'; or 'want' as opposed to 'like'; or '500 grams' as opposed to 'one kilo' as opposed to 'this bunch'; and so on. This kind of meaning forms part of specific individual messages. The meanings relevant to the overall message form are expressed as the structure potential, or GSP, introduced in Chapter 4. For CC1, such meanings are coded as Sale Request, Sale Compliance, Sale Enquiry, and so on.

two general kinds of meaning in a genre-specific semantic potential

See p. 63.

Obviously the two kinds of meaning are related. More specifically, within the range of the former type of meanings are those that, as it were, 'construct' a particular element. So, for example, SR is constructed, or realised, by the following set of meanings: demand some quantity of commodity of the class 'perishable food'. It is at this level of generality that the meanings are relevant to the realisation of the structural element. So far as the identity of SR is concerned, it is not affected by which one of the following we have; each is an adequate realisation of the SR:

1. Can I have a bunch of celery?
2. I'd like two yellowstone peaches.
3. 500 grams of tomatoes and a lettuce, please.
4. I want a really good melon for this evening.

This by no means exhausts the possibilities, but it is obvious that each example realises in some form a demand for some quantity and some commodity of some perishable food.

We can afford to make a very much more specific statement now: the kinds of meaning relevant to the identity of a CC are those expressed in the GSP associated with the CC; these meanings are expressed directly as the meaning of the elements of text structure and indirectly as the meaning without which an element of text structure could not be constructed. It follows that the GSP becomes pivotal in any discussion of the identity of a CC and we may claim that only those values of field, tenor, and mode are defining for the identity of the CC that are motivationally related to the elements of its GSP. If CC has these values, then these elements will appear in any text embedded in this CC; if these elements appear in any text, then these values of the CC can be inferred from it.

I shall first illustrate these points and then, in the following subsection, discuss the implications. For example, let us use CC1 as our starting point. First, assume that the field and tenor values remain exactly as in Table 4.1, but that the mode of CC1 differs from another case, CC2. The mode values of both are presented in Table 6.1. The fact that in CC2 mode is different will affect the obligatory element SC of the structure potential associated with CC1. The label SC is somewhat of a misnomer, since the main job of this element is to promote sale rather than to acknowledge the fact of service performed.

See the discussion on 'The identity of a CC', p. 97.

See Table 4.1, p. 59.

Table 6.1 The modes of two distinct CCs

CC1 mode: Channel: phonic;   medium: spoken; + visual contact;
           language role: ancillary . . .
CC2 mode: Channel: graphic; medium: spoken; − visual contact;
           language role: constitutive . . .

Now if a customer is getting goods by dropping in a written order, the occasion for SC does not exist. The optional element SE is also inapplicable except in the trivial sense of a list being iterative by virtue of being a list! And, again, the optional element SI lacks motivation for occurrence. It is noticeable that in keeping with these changes in the GSP, there is the folk awareness or common feeling that 'dropping in an order' is not the same kind of activity as that of 'going shopping'.

Compare the above situation with Table 6.2, where we again take CC1 as the starting point; we assume exactly the same field and tenor, while introducing one change in mode.

Table 6.2 The mode of another CC

CC3 mode: Channel: phonic; noisy; medium: spoken;
           + visual contact; language role: ancillary

CC3 differs from CC1 by virtue of having a 'noisy channel', i.e. there is some disturbance leading to lack of intelligibility. Now, it would be difficult to substantiate a claim of uniqueness for what we have called CC3, since it is highly unlikely that, with everything else being equal, the GSP associated with CC1 will undergo any change in its obligatory elements as a result of a noisy channel. At most, this may give rise to greater iteration of SEs, but both SE and iteration have already been built into GSP1. The implication is that according to the criteria being offered, the situation labelled CC3 cannot rightfully be given that label: it is simply a variant of CC1.

We can sum up the above discussion as follows: the identity of a CC is defined by that calibration of values which motivates the elements of its GSP; particularly, within the GSP, the obligatory elements and the obligatory sequence are decisive in arriving at this definition. In effect, we are reiterating our earlier assertion in a more formal style, namely, that a situation is defined by the meanings typically associated with it. Through this discussion, I hope, I have made the meaning of meaning more precise by suggesting that in the definition of a CC—a situation type—it is the meanings associated with the obligatory elements of structure and their relation that really count. These represent the lowest common factor across all instances of social activities that could be regarded as belonging to the same situation type, the same CC.

See Hasan (1984d).

It is true that the definition is circular, since the GSP itself was defined as the verbal expression of a CC; but the circularity lies in the nature of the relationship between language and reality. If culture and language have grown up side by side complementing each other, then a culturally recognised occasion of talk—a CC—is bound to be known by the peculiarities of the type of talk associated with it.

The uniqueness of a CC

Before we close this section, it is important to comment on the implications of what has been said above. The attempt to define a unique CC is a search for commonality. A unique CC is a class—a type—of situation. Members of a class are never identical in all respects; they are, by definition, alike in all those respects that characterise the class itself. But, then, no class itself is an immanent category. It is a category we create because it meets some need. The notion of a unique CC as a particular situation type is one such category; we set it up to explain certain phenomena, ignoring others.

From one point of view **all** occasions of talk are alike: each of these is a construct containing the abstractions field, tenor, and mode; and so, to this extent, everything that is a context displays this feature of similarity. But at this primary degree of DELICACY—i.e. detail—the concept cannot be utilised for providing any specific information about textual properties. To do this we need more precise information about the kind of field, tenor, and mode that has gone into the make-up of a situation. But, as I briefly pointed out earlier, each of these variables permits a selection from a large number of alternative values; and these alternatives are capable of being described in varying degrees of detail. It is a particular calibration of alternatives at a particular degree of delicacy that constitutes a contextual configuration. So, in effect, when we debate the question of the uniqueness of a CC, we are actually concerned with establishing some specific point on the continuing scale of delicacy; our question can be paraphrased as: how is that point on the scale of delicacy characterised to which we wish to refer as a CC?

See Chapter 4, p. 55.

The cut-off point that I have suggested is determined by my conception of generic identity; I have argued that we need to go this far and no further in delicacy to establish the identity of a CC, where 'this far' is just far enough to permit the motivation of a GSP. One need not know all the details of a particular situation in order to be able to say what the overall structure of the message form would be. You can teach someone how to write, say, an application, without knowing who the applicant is, or who the grantor, or what specifically the applicant is applying for and what justifications are being put forward for granting the application. But if that is the case, then it would be quite wrong to claim that the genre is different depending on whether the application is, say, for leave of absence, or for travel assistance.

However, to say that this latter distinction is not relevant to the identity of a CC is not to imply that the variation is either unimportant or superficial—simply that whatever aspects of text they might motivate, these are not crucial to that text's generic status. For example, if the fact of the phonic channel being noisy leads to a greater occurrence of SE or if the variation in the value of social distance makes Greeting more probable, this is definitely important, but not crucial to the generic status of the text. We shall have occasion to comment on the specific importance of these later. Here let me point out that the CC is not the end of the story where the notion of context is concerned: to reiterate, it is simply a particular calibration of values frozen at a particular point in delicacy for a particular purpose. Moves in delicacy are essential for explaining other features of texts.

Seen from this point of view, each CC is a 'class' category, whose individual members are themselves lower level classes. Let us refer to these as class 1 and class 2, respectively. Every situation that is a class 2 situation is of necessity also a class 1 situation, just as every act of running, jumping, and walking is an act of motion. We can talk of class 2 situations as variants of class 1. Thus CC1 has many variants.

The inherent variation of context

Variants are created either by a move in delicacy , for example, 'channel: phonic' and further 'noisy'; and/or by alteration of values, for example, 'social distance: near maximal' as opposed to 'social distance: non-maximal'. Either of these sources of variation can lead to a change in the actual structure of the texts as illustrated above; but this is by no means necessary. Either of two things can happen: it may lead to no structural variation whatever or the variation may be such as to shift that particular situation type from, say, CC1 to CC2.

As an example of the first outcome, it is highly unlikely that the actual structure of an application text would vary in correlation with whether the application is for leave of absence or for travel assistance. Equally, the actual structure of a shopping text is not likely to change in correlation with whether we are buying dairy produce or fruit and vegetables. We can all think of many comparable examples. As an example of the second outcome, consider the alternation between the modes of CC1 and CC2. There are criterial differences between the structures associated with the two. In the case of CC2—dropping off an order for goods to be delivered—we might argue that the list is a sort of realisation of SR (remember that Sale Request is an obligatory element of GSP1 associated with CC1). But it would be impossible for us to maintain that the GSP associated with CC2 is identical to GSP1. For one thing, the element Sale Compliance cannot appear; and second, it is important to realise that any SP constructed to meet CC2 must be such as to take care of the discrete temporal staging, which has the effect that each element—if element it is—has to be completely finished before another can begin. So if the list is seen as SR, there is no possibility of overlap between SR and the sale compliance; if the accompanying bill is interpreted as the realisation of the element Sale, then the latter is finished long before Purchase can take place. And there may be no formal realisation of Purchase Closure, other than the cashing of the cheque, if payment is made by cheque. In fact, there is good reason for doubting that these various stages of the activity of 'economic exchange' are productive of one text, or that they should be regarded as stages of the **same** CC. Naturally, there are connections between stages; but so are there connections between what we see as distinct activities. For example, the social activity of teaching students something is quite closely connected to that of examining them in that same subject, but we do not think of these as exactly the same kind of events—at least not till we see them from above, as possibly two manifestations of the context of the transmission of knowledge.

See Table 6.1.

See p. 104.

106

This discussion of alternation of values has been useful. It points to the fact that there is no mechanical way of deciding what kind of variation in the values is capable of creating a new contextual configuration; and, at the moment, the definition provided above appears to be the best. But more importantly, the discussion has focused our attention once again on the inherent variability in contexts. A shift in focus can permit us to view CC1 and CC2 as the same context; a comparable shift in focus can make us view the variants of CC1 as the same context, while from the levels of the variants themselves each might appear as distinct from the other as CC1 and CC2 do from their own level. I hope it is not too facile to say that the fuzziness is 'in the nature of things'. The texture of human social life is dense; the concerns of a community are interconnected. So from one angle, the institution of justice appears quite separate from that of daily family life; but from another, the very continuance of family life is the *raison d'être* for the institution of justice. Situations are permeable. It follows that when we talk about two distinct CCs, there is no necessary implication that their distinction is absolute. After all, CC1 and CC2 have more in common than not. Whenever there are commonalities between two (or more) CCs, it is possible that their structure potential too will display some commonality. The relations both between distinct CCs and between variants of the same CC can be represented graphically as in Figures 6.2 and 6.3. Remember, though, that graphic representation is a metaphor, not a reproduction.

Figure 6.2   Two unique CCs and their commonalities

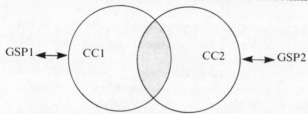

Figure 6.2 shows two distinct CCs, each having a distinct GSP associated with it. The array of actual structures for CC1 would be the realisation of the possibilities captured in GSP1; for CC2, this array would be made up of actual structures permitted by GSP2. The overlapping—shaded—area draws attention to the commonalities between CC1 and CC2. For example, let CC1 be buying vegetables and CC2, buying a car. Obviously a good deal is in common to the field of the two CCs; it is also possible that the social distance may be the same. We would expect that these commonalities of the CC would be reflected in some commonalities across the two GSPs. It is these kinds of comparisons that would allow us to answer questions such as: what is in common to all service encounters?, what is in common to all interactions between non-familiars?, what is in common to all interaction in the spoken mode?, and so on. Though it is hard to imagine any two CCs that would have absolutely nothing in common, the area of overlap is variable: teaching history and poetry have more in common with each other than either has in common with buying vegetables. Let us now look at Figure 6.3.

Figure 6.3 A unique CC and its variants

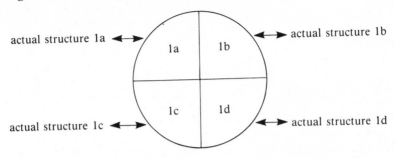

Figure 6.3 shows just one CC, which has just four variants. Each variant is a distinct situation and is associated with an actual structure. However, these actual structures will have many elements in common—in fact all the obligatory elements and their disposition *vis-à-vis* each other.

What counts as one genre?

I raise this question here specifically to remind you that this is one of the issues we wished to examine, but the discussion of the identity of CC has probably resolved the issues already. If you have followed my arguments there, you will anticipate the following comments about genre:

1. A genre is known by the meanings associated with it; in fact the term 'genre' is a short form for the more elaborate phrase 'genre-specific semantic potential'.
2. Genre bears a logical relation to CC, being its verbal expression. If CC is a class of situation type, then genre is language doing the job appropriate to that class of social happenings.
3. Genres can vary in delicacy in the same way as contexts can. But for some given texts to belong to one specific genre, their structure should be some possible realisation of a given GSP.
4. It follows that texts belonging to the same genre can vary in their structure; the one respect in which they cannot vary without consequence to their genre-allocation is the obligatory elements and dispositions of the GSP.

One question that we shall examine later is: can definite statements be made about the linguistic selections in a text type that are genre-motivated, so that every text belonging to a genre would display those linguistic properties? We shall take this question together with that of the identity of a text. Finally we shall raise the question of the pretend-genre of the letter to 'dear Jinny' (Text 6.1).

genres

A text and its uniqueness

Before turning to the central issues of this section, let us first dispose of a fairly minor point. This is the question raised earlier: what is the basis for distinguishing between complete and incomplete texts?

See p. 52.

Again, if you have followed the preceding arguments, you will also see the rationale for wanting to deal with this question first. The answer to this question is implicit in what has been said about the CC and therefore by implication about the genre. The question of a text's completeness can only be answered by reference to the notion of a GSP. A text is perceived as complete if its messages are such that they can be reasonably taken as the manifestation of all the obligatory elements of some one particular SP. So, any text that has messages that could be seen as the realisation of the elements SR, SC, S, P, and PC would be regarded as a complete text belonging to the genre of buying and selling perishable food in face-to-face interaction. We need to add the condition that the obligatory elements of the SP must be realised in some permissible sequence in order for the text to be taken as a well-formed instance of the genre. So the identity and sequencing of the elements of structure form the most reliable basis for making judgments about the completeness and incompleteness of a text. The answer to the first question, then, is in terms of the structural unity, not in terms of the unity of texture.

See pp. 59–61 for a discussion of these symbols.

Does texture play no part in determining whether or not a text is complete? It appears that the relationship is only in one direction: if a piece of language is lacking in texture, then it will either be an incomplete text or a non-text; but the argument does not apply in the opposite direction—something that is fully cohesive does not necessarily represent a complete text. Let me give some examples. Suppose that all we have is *I think I am*; we have no difficulty in saying that this, by itself, could not possibly represent a normal complete text; the elliptical cohesive device of the clause *I am* requires interpretation and it is a type of ellipsis whose interpretation is normally provided verbally. So we need something more to have even a minimal text, something like *Are you invited to Mike's New Year party?*, to which *I think I am* can function as an appropriate answer, concluding a minimal interaction between two participants who are perhaps working in the same room and having intermittent little chats. Imagine, however, that we come across a bit of paper on which is scribbled the following sequence of messages: *Many years ago there was a girl and a boy. They had no mother or father. They had to work for their living*; now these sentences do not 'project' any uninterpreted cohesive devices; yet no one is likely to say that the sequence represents a complete text.

These examples show how texture is not as sure a basis for judgments regarding the completeness of a text as structure is. Let me also draw attention to what is implied in this answer: to say that the notion 'complete text' is explicable by reference to the obligatory elements of a particular SP is to make it dependent upon the notion of genre identification. In effect, then, what one is saying is that the features, the factors, which allow us to judge whether or not a text is complete are

Genre is the verbal
expression of a CC.

essentially the same features that also allow us to identify its register, i.e. genre. This is quite understandable; genre is the verbal expression of a contextual configuration. The overall nature of the social activity not only functions as a motivation for the SP but, in so functioning, provides the basis for determining ideas of completeness.

Levels of textual identity

The discussion of the CC and the genre will have prepared you for the view that the discussion of a text's uniqueness is also the discussion of the ways in which two (or more) texts could be identical. To arrive at a balanced view, we have to keep both differences and similarities in mind simultaneously. There are at least four levels at which these differences and similarities can be perceived.

differences and
similarities in texts

material uniqueness and
verbal identity

First, material uniqueness and verbal identity. This difficult-sounding phrase refers to something you must have often noticed—that we say the same words and sentences on distinct occasions. Let's take a simple example. If on the night of 16 February 1984, while locking the front door, I say to my husband *Did you put the cat out?*, and he says *Yes*, this could be one complete text. Now imagine that next night the same interaction takes place, only this time we are in the kitchen—this too could be regarded as one text. It is distinct from the first one. On a subsequent occasion, it is my husband who asks me the same question and my reply is *Yes*. So we then have a third text. These texts—Cat 1, Cat 2, and Cat 3—have exactly the same set of words and sentences; but we would all think of them as three individual texts. The relation between these three texts is not the same as that between the different copies of this book. If the three Cat interactions are viewed as three distinct texts, this is because each has a different material situational setting; the time and the place of each are different. They are materially unique, though verbally—from the point of view of what words and sentences are used—they are identical. Material uniqueness is the simplest kind of uniqueness that might be used to establish the identity of one text as against another.

verbal uniqueness and
structural identity

The second level may be phrased as verbal uniqueness and structural identity. Consider Texts 6.3 and 6.4.

Text 6.3

C: Can I have ten oranges and a kilo of bananas please? .... ⌉SR
V: Yes, anything else? .... ⌉
C: No thanks. .... ⌉SC
V: That'll be dollar forty. .... ⌉S
C: Two dollars. .... ⌉P
V: Sixty, eighty, two dollars an' thank you. .... ⌉PC

As can be seen from the symbols in the right margin of Texts 6.3 and 6.4, their structure is identical: SR^SC^S^P^PC. However, the words and sentences of the two texts differ from each other. As you would concede quite readily, these two texts must have been produced at least on different occasions; if they were produced at the same time then the

110

Text 6.4

C: Can I have half a dozen Granny Smiths please? ....]SR
V: Anything else? ....]
C: No, that's all just now. ....]SC
V: Ninety cents. ....]S
C: Ninety cents? Oh I think I've just the right change here. ....]P
V: Thank you sir. ....]PC

interactants would be distinct and vice versa. Verbal uniqueness presupposes material uniqueness, but the reverse is not true: every text that is verbally distinct from some other text must have been produced on a unique occasion; but not every material occasion that is unique is necessarily productive of a verbally unique text.

Let us now turn to the third level of differences and similarities between texts. Compare Texts 6.3 and 6.4 with Text 6.5.

Text 6.5

V: Good morning Mrs Reid. ....]
C: Good morning Bob. ....]G
    Can I have a couple of apples? ....]SR
V: Is that all today? ....]
C: Yes, thank you. ....]SC
V: Sixty cents. ....]S
C: Here y'are. ....]P
V: Thank you. ....]PC
    Goo'day. ....]F
C: Bye. ....

The structure of Text 6.5 is G^SR^SC^S^P^PC^F. Neither the words and sentences of Text 6.5 nor its structure is identical with Text 6.3 or 6.4. But is there nothing in common to these three texts? This is obviously a rhetorical question, because you can see that there is a good deal in common to the actual structure of these three texts. This is not surprising; they represent two possible realisations of the same GSP. Structural uniqueness presupposes verbal uniqueness; no two texts that differ in their actual structure can have the same words and sentences altogether. This principle is demonstrated by comparing Text 6.5 with Texts 6.3 and 6.4. But on the other hand, the fact of having the same actual structure does not imply verbal identity, either; this can be seen by comparing Texts 6.3 and 6.4.

Structural uniqueness presupposes verbal uniqueness.

What is common to Texts 6.3, 6.4, and 6.5 is their generic status: they are alike because all three display the criterial properties of GSP1. This point can be made quite clearly by a comparison of Text 6.6 with the others.

See p. 64.

Text 6.6 resembles Text 6.5; but the similarity between these two is of a different kind from that which exists between Texts 6.3, 6.4 and 6.5. Text 6.6 resembles Text 6.7 because both have the elements Greeting and Finis, but as you recall, these elements have an optional status in GSP1; and optional elements are not criterial to the generic status of texts. By contrast, what is common to Texts 6.2, 6.3, and 6.4 is that

Text 6.6

C: Good afternoon, Mr Berg.

B: Oh hello, Mrs Clint. How are you?

C: I'm very well. I um ah I just wan. . .
   I wondered if I could um have a cutting from one of your plants, you know.

B: Oh you're most welcome, m'dear.
   Which one—you just have to say and you can have any you like 'cause y'know I'd be very happy.

C: Oh thank you that's really great um this you know the the those that bush over there the fuschia I love those only I can't . . .

B: Oh but that's very easy I'll set it in for you take 'bout a week—and now any time you wan' anything you just have to say—anything at all.

C: Ah thank you, Mr Berg, that's really kind—and um I shall come over um 'bout a week's time then, shall I?

B: Yes you do that.

C: Well uh see you again, Mr Berg.

B: Yeah be seein' you.

their actual structures contain the obligatory parts of the same GSP. While there is generic identity amongst these three, they are all distinct from Text 6.6 with regard to genre. So Texts 6.5 and 6.6 are generically unique. Generic uniqueness presupposes uniqueness of actual structure—i.e. structural uniqueness.

Thus two texts that are generically unique are also structurally unique—their actual structure will be different. Two texts that are structurally unique will also be verbally unique—the words and sentences of those texts will be different. Two texts that are verbally unique will also be materially unique—the instance of situation, the occasion of talk for them will be different. But it is not possible to claim that if two texts are generically identical then they must be structurally identical; or if two texts are structurally identical, then they must be verbally identical; or if they are verbally identical, then they must be materially identical. By building in inherent variation in the concept of SP and of CC, we have rejected the crude determinism whereby each text and its context are utterly predictive of each other. We have done this by claiming that only certain aspects of texts are sensitive to contexts in a generalisable way.

If the generic uniqueness of a text presupposes uniqueness right down to the first level, then is there nothing in common between two generically unique texts? In answering this question we come full circle to the beginning of Chapter 4: what is in common to them is the most outstanding characteristic of texts in general—their unity, the unity of structure and of texture. But is there any point at which these two kinds of unities come together? I have discussed in great detail how structure and context are related. Could the same be said about texture and context? To answer these questions we must turn to the question of verbal uniqueness.

See p. 52.

Texture, structure, and context

Compared to texture, structure is concerned with the more general—less particular—aspects of a text. So it is possible to talk about the realisation of a structural element in terms of a set of general categories; it is not at all necessary to mention specific items as such. This is one reason why verbal identity is never entailed by structural identity. For example, if we go to CC1, once again, we can say that texts embedded in variants of this context are likely to contain meanings that can be realised by:

See Halliday (1985).

1. Processes—verb words—which are essentially relational, concerned with attribution, for example, *have*, *be*, *see*, *appear*, *cost*, *weigh*, *measure* or a small set of mental processes of reaction which are 'pre-possessive', for example, *want*, *like*, *love*, *care*, and possibly, a few others.
2. Things—noun words—which belong to the class of concrete goods which are organic, edible, and perishable; and another set pertaining to money.
3. Modifiers—descriptive words, for example, adjectives—which can refer to size, quantity, and quality.
4. Interactants—the 'I' and the 'you'—means of referring to self and others in the shop.
5. Message functions will range over the specification of need, demand, giving, describing, finding-out.

I would like to emphasise the fact that what I have been talking about are meanings, not their wording. Of course there is just this problem that—as T.S. Eliot said—'I gotta use words when I talk . . .', and this is so much more true here precisely because we are in a register where the role of language is not ancillary but defining: all of the significant activity is manifestable only through language. So as you read the above lines it might seem to you as if I have been saying nothing but that certain classes of words must occur in any text embedded in any variant of CC1. But in fact, the statement of genre specific 'language' is best given in terms of the semantic categories, rather than the lexico-grammatical ones, since (1) the range of meanings have variant realisation; and (2) the more delicate choices within the general area is not a matter of generic ambience. And both these factors are relevant to texture.

Let me give an example of what I mean by the first rationale given above. First, a particular meaning may be realised lexically and/or grammatically and/or phonologically. Take the notion of 'demand'. We might say *Leave at once* or *I demand that you leave immediately*. Both convey the meaning 'demand', but only the latter has a lexical realisation as well. Even within the area of lexicon, two vectors of variation are possible. I do not have to say to the salesman *I'll have two Granny Smith apples*; I can get by with *Coupla those*, if the apples are there and I have already started off on my list of purchases. Meanings do not have to be encoded explicitly, using what is known as 'fully lexical' items or 'content words'. Take another example: I go to the butcher's and say *Leg of lamb please, usual size*. Here the encoding of

113

'quantity' is implicit; but this time the condition for its appropriate use cannot be stated by reference to the material situational setting. Instead I must look to the contextual configuration, particularly to values in the variable 'tenor': what is the 'social distance' between myself and the butcher? If it is 'non-maximal', it means that I have interacted with this salesperson with some frequency: familiarity does not always breed contempt; it also breeds comfort.

The comfort of knowing what a person is on about increases as the frequency and the variety of types of interaction increase. The implicit expression *usual size* can be interpreted without any problem by a butcher who has been selling me meat with any frequency; so if 'communication' is the name of the game, then restricted exophorics (Hasan, 1984c) of this type can only be used appropriately for the realisation of certain meanings if there is a body of relevant shared experiences between the interactants. These examples highlight the fact that meanings may be encoded either explicitly or implicitly; and that certain kinds of implicitness are appropriate to certain specific contextual values.

The second vector of variation in lexical encoding arises from the distinction between generality and specifity of meaning. The lexical items of a language are variable in specificity; this is the fact that is captured in the hyponymy relation, so *fruit* is less specific than, say, *apple* or *pear*. But *fruit* itself is less general than, say, *thing* (Hasan, 1984c). I do not have to say to a salesman *I want to buy* . . .; I can get away with *I'll have*. . . . The more general the lexical item, the more its meaning in any given instance is conditioned by its generic environment— both contextual and co-textual. In isolation, a question such as *Do you have tea?* would be normally interpreted as an enquiry about the addressee's preference for tea; but in years of shopping, no salesman has yet replied *No, I drink coffee*. This is because in the context of the shopping genre, this question is interpreted as *Does this shop carry tea?*. So variant realisations of the same—in some sense of same—meanings is one reason why generic identity between two texts does not argue for verbal identity.

The areas of meaning such as are specified in our preceding list numbered 1-5, though limited when compared with the total system of language, still represent a vast area for movement. I have pointed out above that so far as the generic status of a text is concerned it makes no difference whether as an instance of thing bought we 'have' a kilo of beans, or a litre of milk. But a text is always embedded in a specific situation as much as it is in a CC. That is to say, certain aspects of a text are determined by the here-and-now-ness of that particular interaction. To this extent, the specific selection of meanings from the wide range permitted is OPPORTUNISTIC; that is, it just so happens that at this time, in this place, this carrier of the dyadic role is focused upon this specific corner of the generic range. So when it comes to the actual unfolding of a text, both the speaker and the addressee must attend precisely to these opportunistically selected meanings, for at the level of **a** text it matters a great deal whether one got a litre of milk when one went out to get it or a kilo of beans! At the level of **a** genre, these opportunistic selections are relevant only to the extent that they are manifestations of a higher order abstraction.

Now, it is these opportunistic selections that are truly the nub of the textural relations in the text. And if you consider the question carefully, you will note that the opportunistic selections are precisely the ones that are governed by highly delicate values of the situation type. Thus the field is not only 'economic transaction: purchase: perishable food' but also 'green grocery: fruit: strawberry'. It is the selection of 'strawberry' that justifies the attributes *ripe* and *sweet* in Text 4.2. Had the customer in Text 4.2 been buying celery or green pepper, these attributes would have been inappropriate. So to put it informally, in the buying of bread, the attributes and the quantity expressions will be decidedly different from those that I need for discussing bananas. And this is the stuff of which cohesion is made: cohesive harmony is not a phenomenon that happens, as it were, independent of what is being done; the difference of one meaning has repercussions for other meanings in the text, and it is the interrelating of meanings that is reflected in cohesive harmony, as I tried to show in the last chapter. What is unique to the text forms the base also of what has to be cohesive. You do not 'peel' 'bread' any more than you look for 'unleavened banana'. It has been said, apropos of dialogues, that as soon as the other person has opened their mouth and said a few words, the possibilities of what you may go on to say become fairly limited. Gregory Bateson (1972) puts the same idea across: 'From what I say it may be possible to make predictions about how you will answer. My words contain meanings and information about your reply'. I am going one step further; I am suggesting that irrespective of whether it is a dialgoue or a monologue, as soon as you have said one word, you have created an environment. The more that is said, the greater the limitations on what can be said relevantly and sensically—and so long as you are being relevant it means you must employ devices that will construct relations of co-referentiality and co-classification as well as lead to the formation of semantic fields. Situation type, at a high degree of specificity, is relevant to texture; you could see it as the motivating force of texture. But by the same token, the facts of texture construe the very detailed aspects of the situation in which the text came to life.

See Table 4.3, p. 61.

When we raise the question of the specific relationship between elements of structure and facts of texture, one interesting finding in recent years has been that the cohesive chains display a close relationship to the structural movement of the text. So far this finding is restricted to two major genre types: fictive narratives (Hasan, Delaware, 1984) and exposition (Martin, 1984). Further research is needed for confirmation of this relation.

A pretend-genre: what does it tell us?

Having examined the question of text, genre, and context identity, we may turn now to the letter addressed to 'Dear Jinny' (Text 6.1). Why do we read this as 'an advertisement composed as if a letter'? There is the obvious structural element of 'address' realised by *Dear Jinny*. The first argument one is tempted to give against its being a letter is the talk about Glo-Quick's Super-Facial.

See p. 98.

One might maintain that this is not the kind of thing one talks about in letters. But, in fact there appears to be no topic or subject-matter restriction in letters written to a close peer or friend. What makes us suspicious is the fulsomeness of the praise and the highly explicit style in which the praise is couched. If Jinny is so close to the writer that she can recommend a beauty treatment and be the recipient of such intimate bits of information as offered in the last sentence of the fragment, it is highly unlikely (1) that the letter would continue without some kind of greeting or other indication of sociability after the address; and (2) that the writer would spell out everything so carefully and (3) so precipitately. The fulsomeness of praise is a well-known attribute of advertisements. Explicitness is essential in the realisation of the Sale, without which the advertisement does not achieve its purpose.

We see then that in determining the genre of a particular text, we tend to examine many features at once. The what, the who, and the how of sayings are at once important; texts do not have discrete realisations of each of these aspects. So while a very delicate specification of field might 'cue' us to a specific area of the lexicon, the equally delicate description of tenor might determine whether the level of the vocabulary has to be formal or informal—whether we need to say *peruse (this) document* or *read (this) stuff*, whether we talk about *spiders* or about *arachnids*. Mode will determine such things as whether certain kinds of implicitness can be interpreted or not; it is no use my saying *Read this stuff* if you cannot see what constitutes 'thisness'. A text has many modes of existence and so it can be analysed at many different levels, with each contributing to our understanding of the phenomena involved.

Coda

Learning through text in context

I set out to establish two major points:

1. the notions of text and context are inseparable; text is language operative in a context of situation and contexts are ultimately construed by the range of texts produced within a community;
2. texts are characterised by the unity of their structure and the unity of their texture.

In Chapters 4 and 5, I attempted to provide some idea of what is meant by structure and texture. This chapter has been concerned with tying both these notions closely to the concept of context and thus showing the logical links between (1) and (2). Much work needs to be done in this area. There is surely no implication here that the details of description provided are above reproach. The work can be examined from two angles: as providing a framework for the study and analysis of texts; and as providing examples of such analysis of specific texts. Obviously, if the validity of the former is doubted, then the latter is also invalidated, but the reverse is not necessarily true. In the description of texts, it is difficult to provide a model that is satisfactory from all points of view. This is not simply because the field is newly revived, but also because the task is immensely demanding and complex. But growth in this area is essential almost as a condition of survival for the study of language. All of us are users of language and we approach it with a commonsense interest in what language can do for us. One commonsense conception is, of course, that our ideas, our knowledge, our thoughts, our culture are all there—almost independent of language and just waiting to be expressed by it. This attitude is so deeply rooted that it finds its expression, for example, in our theoretical writings about language. Nothing makes us see the shortcomings of this approach so effectively as the study of text, for nowhere in the study of language is it so imperative that we clarify our ideas of the relationship between language and the so-called extra-linguistic reality.

There is yet another form of this same misconception that underlies the view that a social activity is just concerned with what passes— quite independent of to whom and how. Again this view is deep-rooted and we tend to think we 'know' what can or cannot be 'said' within

117

one genre or another. And at some level we must know these things, for we participate daily in the unfolding of many a text in many a genre. But what we consciously perceive ourselves as 'knowing' might be rather different from the deeper knowing with which we act with our language. For example, I thought that in the genre of shopping, one would need mainly words that would refer to some set of 'actions'. The study of a few typical interactions in that genre soon put that idea to rest; as I remarked earlier, the majority of verbs belong to a 'descriptive' type rather than 'action' type. Thus interest in text analysis is a good means of making us aware of some of the most glaring misconceptions about language.

Text analysis more than any other interest in language sensitises us to the tenuous nature of the boundary between language and non-language. It throws in doubt the unjustified division between knowing language and knowing how to use language. Teachers in particular are—or at least should be—interested in the appropriate use of language. Places of learning are built around talk, and talk does not consist of 'an infinity of grammatical sentences'. In fact, the dynamics of talk and text can tolerate a good deal of ungrammaticality, potential ambiguity, and what from some points of view might be seen as stylistic infelicity—hummings and hawings, repeating and breaking off. It is helpful to be able to explain what variations in the linguistic form correlate with which contextual value, rather than operate with a rarefied idea of 'a good style', or 'the right sequence of arguments'. The understanding of generic variation, the realisation of the interdependence of text and context, can but assist in these tasks—quite apart from providing many hours of fascination in attempting the analysis of that everyday phenomenon the friendly casual chat, which ostensibly has no goal but underneath which is hidden much of the fabric of any culture.

References

Bateson, G., *Steps to an Ecology of Mind* (Ballantine Books, New York, 1972).

Bauman, R., & Sherzer, J., *Explorations in the Ethnography of Speaking* (Cambridge University Press, London, 1974).

de Beaugrande, R., *Text, Discourse and Process* (Longman, London, 1980).

Bernstein, B., *Class, Codes and Control*, vol. 1 *Theoretical Studies Towards a Sociology of Language*, Primary Socialization, Language and Education (Routledge & Kegan Paul, London, 1971).

Britton, J., *Language and Learning* (Penguin, Harmondsworth, 1970).

Bühler, K., *Sprachtheorie: die Darstellungsfunktion der Sprache* (Fischer, Jena, 1934).

Cazden, C.B., John, V. P., & Hymes, D. (eds.), *Functions of Language in the Classroom* (Columbia Teachers College Press, New York, 1972).

Chomsky, N., *Syntactic Structures* (Mouton, The Hague, 1957).

Christie, F., 'Learning to write: A process of learning how to mean', *English in Australia* **66**, pp. 4−17 (1983).

Cloran, C., *The role of language in negotiating new contexts*, BA (Hons) thesis (Macquarie University, Sydney, 1982).

Culler, J., *Saussure*, Fontana Modern Masters Series (Fontana, London, 1976).

Firth, J.R., 'The technique of semantics', *Transactions of the Philological Society* (1935). Reprinted in J.R. Firth, *Papers in Linguistics 1934−1951* (Oxford University Press, London, 1959).

Firth J.R., 'Personality and language in society', *Sociological Review* **42** (1950), pp. 37-52. Reprinted in J.R. Firth, *Papers in Linguistics 1934−1951* (Oxford University Press, London, 1959).

Fries, P., 'On the status of theme in English: Arguments from discourse', in J. S. Petöfi & E. Sozer (eds.), *Micro and Macro Connexity of Texts* (Helmut Buske, Hamburg, 1983).

Gerot, L., *A question of answers in reading comprehension*, MA (Hons) thesis (Macquarie Univesity, Sydney 1982).

Goffman, E., *Frame Analysis: An Essay on the Organization of Experience* (Harper & Row, New York, 1974).

Goffman, E., *Replies and Responses*, Working Papers & Publications C 46–47 (International Semiotics and Linguistics Centre, University of Urbino, Urbino 1975). Revised and reprinted in E. Goffman, *Forms of Talk* (University of Pennsylvania Press, Philadelphia, 1981).

Goffman, E., *Forms of Talk* (University of Pennsylvania Press, Philadelphia, 1981).

Halliday, M.A.K., *Explorations in the Functions of Language*, Explorations in Language Study (Edward Arnold, London, 1973).

Halliday, M.A.K., *System and Function in Language: Selected Papers*, edited and with an introduction by G.R. Kress (Oxford University Press, London, 1976).

Halliday, M.A.K., 'Text as semantic choice in social contexts', in T.A. van Dijk & J.S. Petöfi (eds.), *Grammars and Descriptions* (W. de Gruyter, Berlin, 1977).

Halliday, M.A.K., *Language as Social Semiotic: The Social Interpretation of Language and Meaning* (Edward Arnold, London, 1978).

Halliday, M.A.K., *An Introduction to Functional Grammar* (Edward Arnold, London, 1985).

Halliday, M.A.K., *Spoken and Written Language* (Oxford University Press, Oxford, 1989).

Halliday, M.A.K., & Hasan, R., *Cohesion in English*, English Language Series 9 (Longman, London, 1976).

Hasan, R., 'Code, register and social dialect', in B. Bernstein (ed.), *Class, Codes and Control*, vol. 2 *Applied Studies Towards a Sociology of Language*, Primary Socialization, Language and Education (Routledge & Kegan Paul, London, 1973).

Hasan, R., 'Text in the systemic-functional model', in W.U. Dressler (ed.), *Current Trends in Textlinguistics* (W. de Gruyter, Berlin and New York, 1978).

Hasan, R., 'On the notion of text', in J.S. Petöfi (ed.), *Text vs. Sentence: Basic Questions of Textlinguistics* (Helmet Buske, Hamburg, 1979).

Hasan, R., 'What's going on: A dynamic view of context in language', in J.E. Copeland & P.W. Davis (eds.), *The Seventh LACUS Forum* (Hornbeam Press, Columbia, SC, 1980).

Hasan, R., 'The structure of the nursery tale: An essay in text typology', in L. Coveri (ed.), *Linguistica Testuale* (Bulzoni, Rome, 1984).

Hasan, R., 'The nursery tale as a genre', *Nottingham Linguistic Circular* **13** (Special Issue on Systemic Linguistics, ed. M. Berry, M. Stubbs, & R. Carter, 1984a).

Hasan, R., 'Coherence and cohesive harmony', in J. Flood (ed.), *Understanding Reading Comprehension* (IRA, Newark, Delaware 1984b).

Hasan, R., 'Ways of saying and ways of meaning', in R. Fawcett, M.A.K. Halliday, A. Makkai & S.M. Lamb (eds.), *The Semiotics of Culture and Language* (Frances Pinter, London, 1984c).

Hasan, R., 'What kind of resource is language?' *Australian Review of Applied Linguistics* **7**(1) (1984b), pp. 57–85.

Hasan, R., *Linguistics, Language, and Verbal Art* (Oxford University Press, Oxford, 1989).

Hymes, D.H., 'Models of the interaction of language and social setting', *Journal of Social Issues* **23** (1967).

Jakobson, R., 'Closing statement: Linguistics and poetics', in T.A. Sebeok (ed.), *Style in Language* (MIT Press & Wiley, Cambridge, Massachusetts 1960).

Lamb, S.M., *Outline of Stratificational Grammar* (Georgetown University Press, Washington, DC, 1966).

Malinowski, B., 'The problem of meaning in primitive languages', Supplement 1 in C.K. Ogden & I.A. Richards (eds.), *The Meaning of Meaning*, International Library of Philosophy, Psychology and Scientific Method, (Kegan Paul, London, 1923).

Malinowski, B., *Coral Gardens and their Magic*, vol. 2 (Allen & Unwin, London, 1935). Reprinted as *The Language of Magic and Gardening* Indiana University Studies in the History and Theory of Linguistics (Indiana University Press, Bloomington, Indiana, 1967).

Martin, J.R., 'Conjunction: The logic of English text', in J.S. Petöfi & E. Sozer (eds.), *Micro and Macro Connexity of Texts* (Helmut Buske, Hamburg, 1983).

Martin, J.R., 'Language, register and genre', in *Children Writing: Reader* ECT412 Children Writing (Deakin University, Victoria, 1984), pp. 21–30.

Martin, J.R., & Rothery, J., 'Writing Report No. 1', *Working Papers in Linguistics*, Department of Linguistics (Sydney University, Sydney, 1980).

Martin, J.R., & Rothery, J., 'Writing Report No. 2', *Working Papers in Linguistics* (Department of Linguistics, University of Sydney, Sydney, 1981).

Mitchell, T.F., 'The language of buying and selling in Cyrenaica: A situational statement', *Hesperis* **26** (1957). Reprinted in T.F. Mitchell, *Principles of Firthian Linguistics*, Longman's Linguistics Library (Longman, London, 1975).

Morgan, J.L., 'Toward a rational model of discourse comprehension', *Theoretical Issues in Natural Language Processing* **2** (1978).

Morris, D., *The Naked Ape* (Jonathan Cape, London, 1967).

Sacks, H., Schegloff, E., & Jefferson, G., 'A simplest systematics for the organization of turn-taking in conversation', *Language* **50** (1974), pp. 696–735.

Schegloff, E., 'Sequencing in conversational openings', *American Anthropologist* **70** (1968).

Ure, J., & Ellis, J., 'Register in descriptive linguistics and linguistic sociology', in O.U. Villegas (ed.), *Issues in Sociolinguistics* (Mouton, The Hague, 1979).

Van Dijk, T.A., *Text and Context: Explorations in the Semantics and Pragmatics of Discourse*, Longman's Linguistics Library (Longman, London, 1977).

Ventola, E.M., 'The structure of casual conversation', *Journal of Pragmatics* **3** (3/4), 1979.

Further reading

Note: the titles are arranged here in an order which roughly follows their relevance to the various chapters of Language, Text, and Context.

Hawkes, T., *Structuralism and Semiotics,* New Accents Series (Methuen, London, 1977).

This book offers an introduction to the study of semiotics. A reading of it will help give an additional understanding useful as a background to exploring the notion of language as a 'social semiotic'.

Culler, J., *Saussure*, Fontana Modern Masters Series (Fontana, London, 1976).

Ferdinand de Saussure (1857–1913) is sometimes referred to as the founder of modern linguistics. The value of this book to students of this course is that in discussing Saussure, Culler provides a sense of the kinds of issues twentieth-century linguistics has attempted to examine, relating these to significant themes and issues in other major twentieth-century social sciences.

Malinowski, B., 'The problem of meaning in primitive languages', Supplement 1, in C.K. Ogden & I.A. Richards (eds.), *The Meaning of Meaning* (Kegan Paul, London, 1923).

This is the essay in which Malinowski introduced and developed his very important notions of 'context of situation' and 'context of culture'—notions which are central to much of the discussion of the whole course on 'Language and learning'.

Hymes, D.H., 'Models of the interaction of language and social setting', *Journal of Social Issues*, vol. 23 (1967).

Here, Hymes provides an account of the model with which he sets out to explain the relationship of language and social situation.

Halliday, M.A.K., *Explorations in the Functions of Language* (Edward Arnold, London, 1973).

A collection of papers in which a number of the issues dealt with in Chapter 2 of *Language, Context, and Text* were explored some years ago.

Halliday, M.A.K., *Language as Social Semiotic: The Social Interpretation of Language and Meaning* (Edward Arnold, London, 1978).

Several of the papers in this collection provide additional perspectives on much of the discussion in Chapters 1–3: 'Language and social man' (Parts 1 & 2), pp.8–35, 211–35 and 'Language and social structure'.

Gregory, M. & Carroll, S., *Language and Situation*, Language and Society Series (Routledge & Kegan Paul, London, 1978).

A short and useful discussion of language and its relationship to social context.

Benson, J.D., & Greaves, W.S., *You and Your Language*, vol. I: *Styles and Dialects*; vol. II: *Meaning is Choice* (Pergamon Press, London, 1984).

Another textbook which provides a new discussion of register and systemic linguistic theory. It is relevant to all chapters of *Language, Context, and Text*.

Goffman, E., 'Primary frameworks', in *Frame Analysis* (Penguin, London, 1974), pp. 21–82.

Goffman, E., 'Replies and Responses', in *Forms of Talk* (University of Pennsylvania Press, Philadelphia, 1981), pp. 5–77.

Goffman was a sociologist with a particular interest in understanding the ways in which human beings structure or 'frame' experience. There is a relationship between his manner of describing such phenomena in both these papers, and the exploration of text and context particularly in Chapters 5 and 6 in *Language, Context, and Text*.

Hasan, R., 'Text in the systemic functional model', in W.U. Dressler (ed.), *Current Trends in Text linguistics* (W. de Gruyter, Berlin, 1978).

A discussion of text structure complementing that in Chapter 4.

Hasan, R., 'The structure of the nursery tale: An essay in text typology', in L. Coveri (ed.), *Linguistica Testuale* (Bulzoni, Rome, 1984).

A discussion of text structure that expands and develops the discussion of structure in Chapter 4.

Ventola, E.M., 'The structure of casual conversation in English', *Journal of Pragmatics*, vol. 3, 1979, pp. 267–398.

As the title suggests, this paper offers a discussion of the structure of casual conversation in a manner which complements the analysis given in Chapter 4 of *Language, Context, and Text*.

Halliday, M.A.K. & Hasan, R., *Cohesion in English* (Longman, London, 1976).

This book is particularly relevant to the discussion in Chapter 5 in *Language, Context, and Text*.

Hasan, R., 'Coherence and cohesive harmony', in J. Flood (ed.), *Understanding Reading Comprehension* (IRA, Newark, Delaware, 1984).

This paper expands the discussion of the texture of the text as developed in Chapter 5 of *Language, Context, and Text*.

123

Hasan, R., 'Ways of saying: Ways of meaning', in R. Fawcett, M.A.K. Halliday, A. Makkai & S.M. Lamb (eds.), *The Semiotics of Culture and Language* (Frances Pinter, London, 1984).

In this paper Hasan sets out to discuss the relationship of culture and language. It is argued that in any culture people will create semiotic styles—ways of saying, being, and behaving. A semantic style is a style of meaning verbally and the semantic style characteristic of a culture will be in keeping with its prevalent semiotic style. The point is discussed in relation to English though in the original it was discussed in relation to Urdu as well. The paper is relevant to Chapters 4, 5, and 6 of *Language, Context, and Text*.

Pugh, A.K., Lee, V.J. & Swann, J. (eds.), *Language and Language Use—A Reader* (Heinemann Educational Books in association with The Open University Press, London, 1980).

A recent collection of papers addressing many aspects of sociolinguistic theory, all of them relevant to educational practice. A good reference book.

Firth, J.R., 'Modes of Meaning', in *Selected Papers of J.R. Firth 1952—59* (Indiana University Press, London, 1968), pp.190—215.

Firth's work as a linguist has been of fundamental importance in the evolution of the theoretical views on language set out in *Language, Context, and Text*. It is appropriate therefore to include at least one paper by Firth. Here, Firth discusses his views on the particular interest of the linguist in meaning: the linguist studies the speaking person in the social process. The reading is relevant to all parts of *Language, Context, and Text*.

Some works in which authors have sought to demonstrate the application of linguistics to educational issues include the following:

Cazden, C., John V.P. & Hymes, D., *Functions of Language in the Classroom* (Columbia Teachers College Press, New York, 1972).

The general series *Explorations in Language Study* edited, by P. Doughty & G. Thornton, and published by Edward Arnold, London.

Technical terms

Acknowledgements

The author and publishers would like to thank the following for permission to reproduce the material below:

p. 76, extract from Robert Frost, 'The Road Not Taken', from *The Poetry of Robert Frost*, edited by Edward Connery Lathem. Copyright 1916 by Holt, Rinehart and Winston and renewed 1944 by Robert Frost. Reproduced by permission of Henry Holt and Company, Inc.

pp. 78–9, extract from Charles Tomlinson, 'Poem', from his *Collected Poems*, Oxford University Press, 1985. Reproduced by permission of Oxford University Press. Copyright Charles Tomlinson.